Dedicated to the truly decent, compassionate and helpful people who make this world a better place.

All Rights Reserved
Copyright © 2017 by C L Whitworth
Cover Design Copyright © 2017 by C L Whitworth

Table of Contents

The Preheat	4
Chef's Notes	5
Hopey-Changey Blackened BBQ Brisket	6
Obstruction Omelette Surprise	8
3 Bean Circus Serenade	10
Black Rye Matters	12
Pipeline Pasta	14
Pigs-In-A-Blanket	16
Pussy-Grabber Stuffed Cod	18
Bernie Badger Stew	20
Wiki-Leek Soup	22
C-Zar Salad	24
Fake News Fries	26
Trump Supporter Steak	28
Deplorable Duck Pie	30
Crockpot Crow	32
Millennial Meltdown	34
Protester Punch	36
Winning Wild Rice Soup	38
Swampwater Martini	40
Mediterranean Mix-Up	42
Fiesta Border Casserole	44
Humble Hummingbird Cake	46
Twitter Tortellini	48
Alternative Swedish Meatballs	50
Hypocrisy Hamburg Heaven	52
Ironic Seafood Salad	54
Low-Bar Blonde Brownies	56
Healthy Hummus Platter	58
420 Green Guacamole Goodness	60
GBLTQ	62
Budget-Cut Baked Beans	64
Reverse Rice Pudding	66
Media Mash-Up	68
Cluster Fudge	70
Cover-Up Casserole	72
Safe-Again Stir-Fry	74
Odd Orange Greens	76
Unintelligible Upside-Down Cake	78
Ridiculous Red Radish Tuna	80
Comedic Cornbread Catfish	82
Delusional Dill Chicken	84
Cyber Smoothie	86
Turmoil Turkey Pinwheels	88
Crispy Chaos Calamari	90
Reprehensible Ravioli	92
Impeachment Cobbler	94
Meanwhile Mojitos	96
Progressives Paradise Pizza	98
Corporate Coalition Coffee	100
Whirled Peas	102
Wrap Up	104
The Boil Down	106

Introduction

I created this project during a very tumultuous time. I would like this writing to be considered historic, educational, unbiased and objective – with a dash of 'tongue in cheek'. The observations are of the current social climate in the United States–more specifically, the 2016 Presidential Election and just six months thereafter.

This book will expose and examine behavioral patterns honestly and objectively. Facts, actual events, as well as opinions and possible solutions to societal problems will be discussed. You may discover something new, something that conflicts with your current state of understanding or thee best recipe this side of the 'Mississip.' If nothing else, I am sure you will, at least be outraged, offended, embarrassed, and/or enlightened at one point or another.

Appetizer

Politics of the past few years has been, for lack of a better term, "business as usual." It has been contentious at times, but for the most part, standard procedure, with each side trying to gain some ground – within the bounds of normalized ethics and procedures.

There have been several recent events that left a mark on the face of this great nation. The Timothy McVeigh Federal building bombing, the Bush Era Recession (October 2007), which some have still not fully recovered. The Desert Storm wars based on falsified intel, several mass shootings killing dozens, the Bundy stand-off on federal property, several church burnings and shootings by white supremacists terrorists, but '911' (Sept 11, 2001) trade center twin tower attacks remains to be the most notable.

Within the Obama era, we witnessed a practice called, 'Obstructionism', where members of an opposing party, say "NO" to everything presented by the President, "whether it hurts the American people or not." This behavior had not recently been seen, and you can draw your own conclusions as to why this tactic was utilized for the Obama administration.

Republicans can be summed up as preferring to spend money on military and fossil fuel production while de-funding community services, healthcare, education with tax cuts to the rich. Democrats have preferred the opposite, stating we already have more military than any other nation and investing in renewable (clean) energy, education and healthcare would be the most beneficial. Republicans want less government regulations and less oversight in business operations, the EPA and individual choices (except for other people's sexual orientation, equal rights and women's reproductive choices).

The Obama administration won the 2008 election with both the electoral college and the popular vote, on the message of **"Hope and Change."** Emotional crowds burst out in gleeful tears of joy, hugging and singing as the new presidency was announced. If you were a part of that crowd, you felt an instant connection to those across the nation who had been suffering with the previous presidency and all that it had entailed. If you were against Obama and everything he stood for, you felt immediately oppressed and remained that way throughout the entire two terms (according to some people).

At the end of the Obama Administration's two terms (8 years), some of us were happy that equal rights for everyone were defended, environmental protection was enforced and the **Obamacare/Affordable Health Care Act** was introduced to help people (especially with pre-existing conditions) attain healthcare. The wave of foreclosures from the devastating Bush era recession was lessened, allowing people to keep their homes, with lowered monthly payments. The **Wall Street Reform Act** was implemented, to help keep corporations in-check and **incentives for Renewable Energy** start-ups were introduced. But some people became disappointed at what they considered to be a lack of progress. Although the economy grew stronger, some rural communities and coal mining communities were still struggling with huge debt and low or no income/jobs in their area. Due to lack of voter participation, and the Electoral College, the 45th President of the United States was elected with approximately 1/4 of US citizens vote.

The Preheat

From the fire to the frying pan

A thick line was drawn between the Republicans and the Democrats. The points-of-view were on opposite ends of the spectrum—polar opposites, with neither side budging.

New, lower-level ethics reared its ugly head and encouraged rude and unprofessional, even violent behavior, in public forums. Incessant interruptions, personal attacks, heckling and shouting-out of profanities from the audience was becoming 'a thing.'

Early Spring of 2016, we hear of Dakota Pipeline protests by the "Water Protectors," numerous earthquakes in Oklahoma, unexpected celebrity deaths, the break-up of America's favorite celebrity couple, "BradJolena" or whatever their name was...and half of the world was shocked at the lack of qualified or even likable presidential candidates. The fact that Donald Trump tossed his hat into the ring wasn't a big surprise and he more or less, fit-in with the rest of the GOP candidates. Trump's candidacy upped the ante for entertainment ratings for broadcast news and talk show hosts.

By late July, however, divides grew deeper as a new minority group made itself known—the Trump Supporters. The Trump Supporters sported their red baseball caps and t-shirts proudly and loudly. Violence often broke out at national rallies. Townhall meetings became shouting matches and required the presence of law enforcement. The GOP candidates were chewing each other's legs off, like hyenas while the Democratic party was gaining momentum but unwittingly, splitting in half. The Bernie Sanders movement was gaining support... a lot of support. Stadiums were filled. The outcry for a progressive platform was incredible and undeniable but the DNC chose to back Hillary Rodham Clinton (HRC).

>Enter, **'Fake News'** and the Clinton email snafu. The perfect storm of incompetencies, email storage protocol and untimely investigations...it all added up to, 'much ado about nothin' - but it cost HRC the election. With lingering credibility issues and absolutely no charisma, the email situation, mixed with a plethora of truly fake news 'trumped' HRC's 30 years of experience and leadership. Although Clinton won the popular vote with an excess of nearly 3 million votes, fake news, showmanship and apathy were the main ingredients for an all-you-can-eat bizarre buffet.

Chef's Notes

About this Book: The content was captured in 'real time' during a very unusual election and presidency. The United States and the world were shocked and amazed at the outrageous antics and level of political professionalism, or lack thereof.

Most people fall within the 'norms' of social behavior and attitudes. They are reasonable, cooperative and respect the agreed upon laws of society, so that we can all live a fairly decent life. This book contains instances of the beginnings of what may become a subtle shift from decent 'social norms' to... something else.

The main purpose of this book is to bring together supposedly opposing parties to gain insight, understanding and if nothing else, come to the table with a sense of commonality with something everybody can relate to and appreciate—food.

I am not a "food person" so to speak. As a matter of fact, I rarely follow recipes and I never even watch cooking shows. I do, however realize the social value and importance of the proverbial "breaking bread" together. Sharing a meal extends an offer of communism – a sense of community, acceptance and belonging. It's a strong gesture, not to be underestimated. I invite people from all walks of life, all viewpoints and ideals to sit down and partake, participate and prepare one or two of these delightful dishes. Share a recipe, share some food, share some ideas, share some viewpoints, compassion and understanding.

About the Recipes: The recipes, for the most part, are to be taken with a 'grain of salt', so to speak. I do not consider myself to be a connoisseur of any sort, but I am pretty sure all of the recipes are at least somewhat valid, nutritious and safe when used in moderation.

About the Content: The content was captured from the "daily harvest," as I called it. The newsfeeds yielded a plethora of tasty morsels on a regular basis. I will not deny that this project was cathartic. It was a positive way to process the current events. The direction of the country was about to change. I wanted to capture the transition; understand the points of view and hopefully bring people together with insight and understanding.

Disclaimer: I attained most of the content from online newsfeeds. I tried to give credit to the original artist and journalists Contact me, to cite or remove works not properly cited. This book uses generalities and is intended to be used for educational, historical and sometimes satirical purposes.

Hopey-Changey Blackened BBQ Brisket

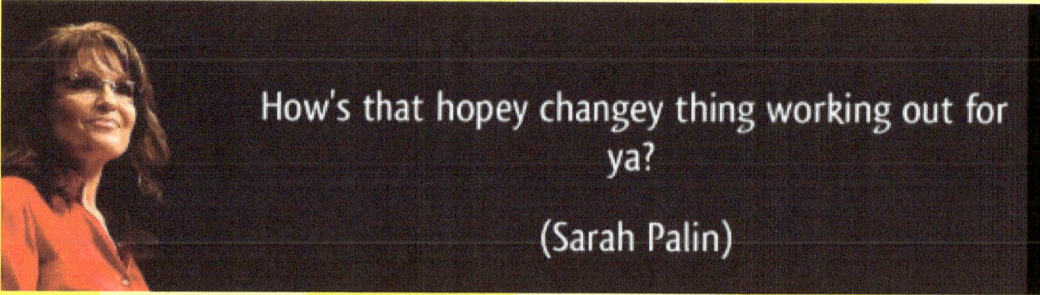

By ALEXANDER BURNS 09/21/11 06:44 AM EDT [POLITICO]

President Barack Obama borrowed a phrase from one of his harshest opponents last night, telling supporters at a New York fundraiser that "all that hopey changey stuff" from the 2008 campaign "was real." The "hopey changey" term comes from a certain former Alaska governor and 2008-vintage Obama opponent. At a tea party convention in Nasvhille last year, Sarah Palin said she wanted to ask Obama's supporters: "How's that hopey changey thing working out for ya?"

Obama's belated response went like this, according to last night's pool report from the Gotham Theater: "All that hopey changey stuff, as they say? That was real. It wasn't something …it was real, you could feel it. You know it. It's still there. Even in the midst of this hardship. But it's hard. When I was in Grant Park that night, I warned everybody this was going to be hard, this wasn't the end it was the beginning." "Over the past 2 and a half years," he said, "the hope poster starts fading. But I tell you what, you travel around the country and talk to the American people, that spirit's still there." In a way, the combination of reviving good feelings from 2008 and spotlighting Palin-like bogeymen who scare independent voters is a decent snapshot of the Democrats' 2012 strategy at this point.

Obama was right. It wasn't going to be easy but there was progress. The wave of foreclosures was greatly lessened. Our auto industry was saved and is now flourishing with more efficient hybrid options. The stimulus bill helped to jump-start the badly broken economy. Obamacare attempted to address the high cost of healthcare and help those with pre-existing conditions to gain coverage. Corporate regulations were increased to help protect employees, consumers and the environment. Infra-structure repair and development was a big focus as well as deeming huge areas of ocean and wildlife land, to be federally protected.

Hopey-Changey Blackened BBQ Brisket

Ingredients

2 pounds Beef Brisket, trimmed
1/4 cup Molasses
1/2 Hickory Smoke BBQ sauce
3 tablespoons Worcester sauce

2 teaspoons Smoked Paprika
2 teaspoons dried Oregano

Directions

It's slow-going! Can't rush this Hopey-Changey Blackened Brisket. Perfect for when you have a lot of time on your hands!

Cut several 1/4-inch-deep slits into brisket. Combine all other ingredients in a large heavy-duty zip-top plastic bag; add brisket. Seal and marinate in refrigerator 8 hours, turning bag occasionally.

Preheat oven to 325°
Remove brisket from bag, reserving marinade. Heat oil in a large oven-proof Dutch oven over medium-high heat. Add brisket; cook 4 minutes on each side or until browned.

Cover and bake in the oven at 325° for 3 hours.

Some Key Hopey-Changey Items:

- Affordable Healthcare
- Wall Street Reform (banker regulations)
- Equal Rights and Equal Pay
- Environmental Protection Regulations (EPA)
- Green Energy Technology Leader

Republicans generally aren't interested in anything the Obama Administrations wants to accomplish; wall street reform, green energy technology, equal rights/pay, stopping foreclosures, healthcare, etc.

Democrats were over-joyed at the prospect of ending the recession and the war and looked forward to infra-structure development, affordable healthcare, renewable energy and higher EPA standards.

Obstruction Omelette Surprise

"The single most important thing we want to achieve is for President Obama to be a one-term president."
— Senate Minority Leader Mitch McConnell, as quoted in the National Journal, Nov. 4, 2010.

"Their [the Democrats] story line is that there must be some villain out there who's keeping this administration from succeeding."
— McConnell on CNN's "State of the Union," Oct. 23, 2011.

"Block Obama At All Costs!"

Here's John Boehner, the likely speaker if Republicans take the House, offering his plans for Obama's agenda: "We're going to do everything — and I mean everything we can do — to kill it, stop it, slow it down, whatever we can."

Senate Minority Leader Mitch McConnell summed up his plan to National Journal: **"The single most important thing we want to achieve is for President Obama to be a one-term president."**

Obama frequently reminds voters he believes all the delay in Washington this year is the Republicans' fault. "So I hope that my friends on the other side of the aisle are going to change their minds going forward, because putting the American people back to work, boosting our small businesses, rebuilding the economic security of the middle class, these are big national challenges. And we've all got a stake in solving them. And it's not going to be enough just to play politics. You can't just focus on the next election. You've got to focus on the next generation," Obama said at a recent event in Rhode Island.

Expecting to work with a head-strong but mature and reasonable associates, Obama spoke of "reaching across party lines" to come up with bi-partisan solutions for an ailing American economy, peoples and environment by imposing corporate regulations, EPA standards, green energy incentives, equal rights and pay for all. The GOP made it clear to all of its members—Block any and all of the President's actions whether its good for the American people or not.

The Party of No: New Details on the GOP Plot to Obstruct Obama

By Michael Grunwald @MikeGrunwald   Aug. 23, 2012

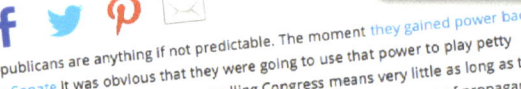
John Boehner Admits Republicans are Willing to Put U.S. at Risk to Play Partisan Politics (Video)

February 16, 2015 By Allen Clifton   59 Comments

Republicans are anything if not predictable. The moment they gained power back in the Senate it was obvious that they were going to use that power to play petty partisan politics. The truth is, controlling Congress means very little as long as the person in the White House has veto power. So no matter what sort of propaganda Republicans spew about the nonsense they're going to undoubtedly shove through Congress, it's still on them to send the president legislation that they know he will sign, otherwise they're essentially just wasting time.

FUN FACT

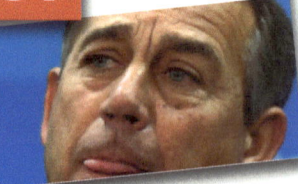

Obstruction Omelette Surprise

Ingredients

- 3 large Eggs
- 1/2 cup shredded Cheddar
- 1/2 Green Pepper, diced
- 1/4 cup Yellow Onion, diced
- 1/4 cup Tomato, diced
- 1/4 cup Sausage, diced
- Garlic powder
- fresh Oregano or Basil
- Olive oil

This delicious bundle of joy will surely block most passages

Directions

Dice everything up. Scramble 3 eggs, pour into medium heat non-stick frying pan. Add shredded cheese, let it melt almost all of way through, then add diced ingredients on half of egg and cheese.
Gently fold over, then sprinkle with garlic, oregano, fresh basil to taste.

Note: Use extra cheese to attain all of that extra blockage you desire.

FUN FACT

Go to https://www.democraticwhip.gov/content/just-facts-house-republicans-record-obstruction to see a list of the issues that Republicans walked out on (figuratively and literally).

Some Accomplishments (despite the blockage):

- Economic Recovery (Stimulus Plan)
- Home Foreclosure Prevention
- Affordable Healthcare (Obamacare)
- Wall Street Reform (Corporate Financial Regulations)
- Environmental Protection Regulations & Standards Increased
- Green Energy Technology Business Incentive programs
- Michelle Obama's Healthy Heart & Lunch Programs
- New Wildlife Preservation Areas
- National Debt Down, Unemployment down

One thing is for sure - The "Bro-mance" is moving on.

Republicans are OK with obstructionism aimed at Obama, as well as closing down the government (while Congress gets paid). "Block Obama at all costs!"

Democrats were hoping for bi-partisan compromises to help the country after the devastating recession and on-going war. They think obstructionism is unpatriotic and damaging to the nation as a whole.

3 Bean Circus Serenade

Republicans to the rescue!

"Look at those hands, are they small hands?" the front-runner for the GOP presidential nomination said, raising them for viewers to see. "And, he referred to my hands -- 'if they're small, something else must be small.' I guarantee you there's no problem. I guarantee."

Rubio in recent days revived a decades-old old insult, mocking Trump for having relatively slight hands.

Here are a few of the most memorable lines. *Trump on his hands and other body parts:* "Look at those hands, are they small hands? And, he referred to my hands -- 'if they're small, something else must be small.' I guarantee you there's no problem. I guarantee."

Trump on Florida Sen. Marco Rubio: *"This little guy has lied so much about my record."* Cruz hits Trump for past support of politicians: "For 40 years, Donald has been part of the corruption you're angry about."

Ohio Gov. John Kasich on why he stays out of the mud on debate nights: *"I have never tried to go and get into these kind of scrums that we're seeing here on the stage and people say everywhere I go, 'you seem to be the adult on the stage.'"*

Rubio on why he decided to insult Trump on the trail: *"For the last year Donald Trump has mocked everybody with personal attacks. He has done so to people sitting on the stage today. He has done so about the people who are disabled. He has done it about with every candidate in this race. If there is anyone that has deserved to be attacked that way, it's Donald Trump for the way he has treated people in the campaign."*

3 Bean Circus Serenade

Ingredients

- 1 can Green Beans
- 1 can Yellow Wax Beans,
- 1 can Red Kidney Beans,
- 1 cup chopped Onion
- 1 cup chopped Green Bell Pepper
- 1 (4 oz) jar chopped Pimento Peppers, drained
- 1/2 cup Vinegar
- 1/2 cup Vegetable Oil
- 1/4 cup White Sugar

Enjoy this colorful, crazy mix!

Directions

Mix green beans, yellow wax beans, kidney beans, onion, celery, green bell pepper, and pimento peppers in a bowl.

Combine vinegar, oil, sugar, salt, and pepper in a saucepan; bring to a boil. Cook and stir until sugar is dissolved, about 5 minutes. Remove saucepan from burner and pour dressing over bean mixture; toss to coat. Refrigerate until flavors blend, 8 hours to overnight.

Republican Agenda

- Increased Coal and Oil Fracking
- Heavy Cuts to Medicaid/Medicare
- Cuts to Public Education
- Not Equal Rights for all
- No Gun Control
- Cut Community Programs
- Infrastructure Funding
- Military Weapons Spending (a lot)

Democratic Agenda

- Green Energy (technology & incentives)
- Healthcare (affordable or free)
- Education (school loan relief/free vocational)
- Equal Rights/Pay for everyone
- Gun Control (bkgd checks, no auto assault)
- Community Programs Funding
- Infrastructure Funding
- Maintain Military (not increase)

Republicans cheer for anyone who will "say what needs to be said" and free them from (what they feel has been) years oppression and "heavy corporate regulations that hinder their creativity" under Obama.

Democrats see the Republican candidates as a collection of unqualified and a backwards thinking group, at best.

Pussy-Grabber Stuffed Cod

"Grab 'em by the pussy"

The Republican nominee for President of The United States, Donald Trump, has been caught on video bragging about sexually assaulting women.
In the video, Trump says that if you are famous "you can do anything" to women, including "grab them by the pussy."

Trump also said that, when he saw a beautiful woman, he didn't seek permission before getting physical. "I don't even wait," he said.

This has prompted a reaction from many of the Republican politicians who have endorsed Trump. In statements, various Republican elected officials have condemned Trump's comments. They used words like "unacceptable," "offensive," and "disturbing." These statements seem warranted but also obvious. Trump Supporters are not fazed and some see it as a comical event and/or a signal to support the abusive behavior.

Deplorablewarpig
@redwarpig

I can't forgive Trump because I see no reason for it. I like men to be men. If I wanted a pussy as my partner I'd be a lesbo.
8:53 AM - 8 Oct 2016

Mean Farmer
@mean_farmer

I don't get why the #TrumpTapes is such a big deal? I like him even more now, if this is the worst thing he's ever done.
6:42 AM - 8 Oct 2016

Amber Jamieson, Simon Jeffery and Nicole Puglise
Thursday 27 October 2016 18.13 EDT

FUN FACT

At least 24 women have accused the Republican presidential nominee, Donald Trump, of inappropriate sexual behavior in multiple incidents spanning the last 30 years.

Pussy-Grabber Stuffed Cod

Ingredients

- 2 fillets of Cod
- 1 Box Stuffing
- 2 Tbsp Olive Oil
- Garlic Powder
- Paprika
- Oregano

An unforgettable, quick and easy dish!

Directions

Preheat the oven to 400 degrees
Lightly grease a 9x13 inch baking dish or use foil. Prepare stuffing and set aside.
Lay the Cod fillets in the prepared baking dish. Brush each one with melted olive oil or butter. Place a heaping tablespoon of the stuffing on each fillet, and fold the other half over to cover. Secure with toothpicks if desired. Sprinkle any remaining stuffing, and drizzle with leftover melted butter. Bake for 20 minutes in the preheated oven until the top has browned and the fish flakes easily with a fork.

OCTOBER 8, 2016

These People Applauding Donald Trump's 'Grab Em By The Pussy' Comments Prove Deplorables Are Real

By **Jacob Geers**   2 Comments

Sep 2016
Keep talking Donald. Wow. I still can't believe anyone could think this guy is fit to even have a drivers license #USPresidentialDebate

Republicans may or may not like the 'grabber' behavior but it didn't stop them from voting for Trump and his values – for some, it actually strengthened the appeal.

Democrats thought this was election-blasting news that would fly in the face of 'Republican Family Values.' They were wrong.

Bernie Badger Stew

Corporations, Pay Your Fair Share and Give Back to the Community That Built You!

Socialism:
It is what we've been doing all along to some degree, with social security, public schools, police, fire departments, US Postal Service, Medicare and Medicaid ...but don't let the facts get in the way of a good story.

The Bernie Sanders movement was a powerful and emotional force grounded in social justice and equality. **Corporations paying their fair share instead of using tax loop-holes was an important part of the solution.** There was a lot of work to be done and Bernie was ready to take the bull by the horns.

 Bernie Sanders @SenSanders · 22h
There's no state where a full-time minimum wage worker can afford a one-bedroom apartment at the fair market rent. That's unacceptable.

 Bernie Sanders @SenSanders · 23h
Every American, regardless of income, must have the right to a higher education.

Bernie Badger Stew

Ingredients

- 1 lb Beef
- 3 medium Red Potatoes
- 1 pkg Onion Soup Mix
- 1 Onion
- 2 Carrots
- 1 cup Peas
- 3 tsp Worcester Sauce
- 1 tablesp Olive Oil
- 1 tsp Flour
- Ground Sage
- Garlic Powder

Good & wholesome! Just what you need to keep you going during those cold protests & rallies.

Directions

Place meat in slow cooker. In a small bowl mix together the flour and seasonings; pour over meat, and stir to coat meat with flour mixture. Worcestershire sauce, onion, beef broth, potatoes, carrots, and peas. Cover, and cook on Low setting for 10 to 12 hours, or on High setting for 4 to 6 hours.

Cut the carrots into small pieces and add them to the pan, along with a splash of red wine or stout (optional). Place the lid on the pan, then bring to boil. Simmer gently for approx. 60 minutes, or until cooked, removing the lid for the last 30 minutes. Add some extra water if necessary for consistency.

While this is cooking, enjoy a nice smooth brandy or weed of your choice... you're gonna need it.

Some nations that currently provide Universal Healthcare:

Australia • Austria • Belgium
Canada • Chile • Denmark
France • Germany • Greece
Israel • Italy • Japan •
Norway • Korea • Spain
Sweden • UK

FUN FACT

"Remember we are still the only major country to not guarantee health care to all its people.

Republicans reject the idea of Universal Healthcare and "Socialism" and want the government to provide LESS for the people, not more.

Democrats want the government to continue providing education, Medicare/Medicaid, Planned Parenthood, law enforcement, fire prevention, postal offices, arts & sciences programs, etc.

Wiki-Leek Soup

Emails on private server leaked just days before election
By Editorial Board November 6, 2016 Washington Post

We have written a lot in recent months about why Mr. Trump is manifestly unqualified — by experience, temperament and outlook — for the Oval Office. We agree that attention paid to his unfitness is to Ms. Clinton's benefit. But we also believe that fair examination of Ms. Clinton in her own right provides convincing evidence that she is well prepared and fully capable to succeed as president of the United States.

When we endorsed Ms. Clinton, we stressed we were not choosing between the lesser of two evils. "Hillary Clinton," we wrote, "has the potential to be an excellent president. . . . Anyone who votes for her will be able to look back, four years from now, with pride in that decision." Not only has Ms. Clinton sketched out a thoughtful and ambitious policy agenda but she has run an impressive campaign, including her choice of running mate and her nimble mastery of three debates.

"I love wikileaks!" ~Donald Trump

FUN FACT

Donald Trump calls on Russia to find Hillary Clinton's missing emails ...
www.vox.com/2016/7/27/.../donald-trump-russia-hack-hillary-clinton-email-dnc ▼
Jul 27, 2016 - "**Russia, if you are listening**, I hope you are able to find the 33000 emails that are missing," **Trump** said.

One of the nations most qualified presidential candidate ever, HRC offers 30+ Years as Public Service/Civil Rights Defender and Former Secretary of State.

Wiki-Leek Soup

Ingredients

- 3 tablespoons Olive Oil
- 1 small Onion, diced
- 3 large Leeks, sliced
- 5 medium Russet Potatoes
- 2-3 cloves of Garlic, minced
- 1 teaspoon dried Thyme
- 1/2 teaspoon dried Rosemary
- 5 cups Vegetable Broth
- 1 Bay Leaf
- 1 1/2 tbsp Lemon Juice
- 1 cup canned Coconut Milk (or any unsweetened plant-based milk)

Wiki-Leek Soup goes nicely with C-Zar Salad

Directions

Make sure leeks are washed well.
Heat the oil in a large pot, over medium heat. Add a pinch of salt to the oil.
Add the leeks & onion, sauté until softened, about 3-5 minutes
Add the potato, garlic, salt, pepper & spices (except the bay leaf). Sauté to release the flavors of the garlic & spices, about 2-3 minutes. Stir often to keep vegetables from sticking. (if it starts to stick, add a touch of oil or vegetable broth)
Add the vegetable broth & bay leaf, bring to a boil. Reduce heat to a low simmer and cook for about 15-20 minutes, or until the potatoes are tender. You can pierce them with a fork to test for tenderness.

Remove from heat and remove bay leaf.
Add the cream and lemon juice.
Using a blender, blend until smooth and creamy. Before blending, set aside a few pieces of potato for the garnish. Serve in soup bowls and top with chopped green onion, fresh ground pepper and a few pieces of cooked potato.

FUN FACT

Pence used a private email server for his emails while serving as Indiana Governor

---

Republicans think Hillary Clinton should be in prison for her email/server situation - even though the FBI has found no damaging emails. Despite her long list of qualifications and experience, they consider her to be corrupt and want to "Lock Her Up!"

Democrats acknowledge the error of both parties using personal servers and accept the FBI's final assessment. Some don't like her corporate ties but realize HRC is far and away the best candidate for the US presidency.

C-Zar Salad

"I Have Nothing To Do With Russia!"

For the past three months reports of connections between **Trump and Putin** have flooded the airwaves. Speculation of possible business deals, indebtedness, coercion, campaign support and even "golden showers" made headline news and leading talk show topics. While these issues seemed to be important to most people, Trump supporters didn't bat an eye.

FUN FACTS

June 18, 2013 - After announcing his annual pageant would be held in Russia, Trump, then a private businessman, tweets, "Do you think Putin will be going to The Miss Universe Pageant in November in Moscow - if so, will he become my new best friend?"

September 2015 - The FBI informs the Democratic National Committee that a Russian-linked cyber-spy group had likely compromised its computer network.

July 22, 2016 - Emails among DNC members favoring Secretary Hillary Clinton over Sen. Bernie Sanders are leaked via Wikileaks. Five days later, Trump explicitly calls for Russia to hack Clinton for further information: "I will tell you this, Russia, if you're listening, I hope you're able to find the 30,000 emails that are missing."

August 14, 2016 - The New York Times reports that $12.7 million in clandestine cash payments have been earmarked for Trump campaign manager Paul Manafort by a pro-Russia Ukrainian political party. The next week it is reported by CNN that Manafort's former firm is being investigated for ties to corruption in the Russian government, and Manafort resigns.

October 7, 2016 - For the first time, the U.S. intelligence community calls out Russia on its ongoing attempts to interfere with the U.S. presidential election. "We believe, based on the scope and sensitivity of these efforts, that only Russia's senior-most officials could have authorized these activities," the report states.

December 1, 2016 - CNN reports that Paul Manafort is once again in Trump's close personal orbit and helping with the transition team.

December 19-28, 2016 - General Michael Flynn, Trump's national security advisor, talks several times with Russian ambassador Sergey Kislyak, reportedly about non-state issues.

December 29, 2016 - President Obama announces that he is imposing new sanctions against Russia and expelling more than 30 of the country's diplomats from Washington. The same day, Flynn and Kislyak speak several times about the sanctions. Since Trump is not yet president, these talks can be construed to constitute a treasonous act.

January 6, 2017 - A U.S. Intelligence report states that Russian President Vladimir Putin ordered a cyber campaign to help Donald Trump beat Hillary Clinton in the presidential election.

January 26, 2017 - The Justice Department warns the Trump administration about Flynn being compromised by Russia, and that the likelihood of Flynn being blackmailed by Russian agents presents a security threat. Trump does not acknowledge the warning until February 14, when he forces Flynn to resign.

C-Zar Salad

Ingredients

- 2 Garlic cloves, minced
- 1 tsp Anchovy Paste
- 2 tsp Lemon Juice
- 1 tsp Dijon Mustard
- 1 tsp Worcestershire sauce
- 1 cup Mayonnaise
- 1/2 cup grated Parmesan
- 1/2 shaved Parmesan
- 1/4 tsp Salt
- 1/4 tsp Black Pepper
- 1 head Romaine Lettuce washed and torn into bite-sized pieces
- 2 cups Croutons

C-Zar Salad goes nicely with Wiki-Leek Soup

Directions

In a medium bowl, whisk together the garlic, anchovy paste, lemon juice, Dijon mustard and Worcestershire sauce.
Add the mayonnaise, Parmesan salt and pepper. Mix it all together and be sure to cover it all up - the romaine lettuce, that is.

Short Version: Those ready-made salad kits in the produce department are pretty good, get the Caesar Supreme.

 Donald J. Trump ✓
@realDonaldTrump   [Follow]

Russia has never tried to use leverage over me. I HAVE NOTHING TO DO WITH RUSSIA - NO DEALS, NO LOANS, NO NOTHING!

5:31 AM - 11 Jan 2017

The Moscow Ritz Carlton episode involving TRUMP reported above was confirmed by Source E, ▮▮▮▮▮▮ who said that s/he and several of the staff were aware of it at the time and subsequently. S/he believed it had happened in 2013. Source E provided an introduction for a company ethnic Russian operative to Source F, a female staffer at the hotel when TRUMP had stayed there, who also confirmed the story. Speaking separately in June 2016, Source B (the former top level Russian intelligence officer) asserted that TRUMP's unorthodox behavior in Russia over the years had provided the authorities there with enough embarrassing material on the now Republican presidential candidate to be able to blackmail him if they so wished.

Russian spy ship spotted off of US coast - C▮▮▮▮▮om

www.cnn.com/videos/.../russia-spy-ship-off-delaware-jpm-orig.cnn
Feb 15, 2017
This is the farthest north the Russian spy vessel has ever ventured, according to US defense official.

Republicans applaud Trump's accusations concerning HRCs emails and chant, "Lock her up!"

Democrats feel the email leak was a Trump/Russian choreographed strategy to influence the election in his favor.

Fake News Fries

Fake News Is A Real Problem!

by Mark Hachman, Senior Editor PCworld

It was only a few minutes after my imaginary Trump supporter "Todd White" began exploring Facebook that he learned filmmaker Michael Moore was staging a coup d'etat against president-elect Donald Trump. Todd also learned that Trump won the popular vote. And that there were people paid to protest at Trump rallies. None of that is true, of course. That's the sort of fake news that's being disseminated by Facebook—bogus content that many believe was written by partisan groups to influence the election.

Questions about Facebook's role in spreading fake news were raised almost as soon as Trump shocked the world with his victory. BuzzFeed and other news sites began publishing reports about how a small town in Macedonia turned fake election news into an industry.

FUN FACT

It appears the authors behind the fake news reports had no partisan agenda. They were just in it for the money. One creator claimed he could make $10,000 per week in ad revenue from stories that were shared among Trump supporters. Democrats didn't buy into nearly as much and therefore weren't worth the effort.

The Macedonians may still be at it, because our Republican supporter, Todd White, was flooded with partisan posts. Worse, over a little more than two days, we counted 10 such posts in his feed that were fake, most accusing Democrats or their supporters of illegal activity. In all, White was clearly exposed to more spin than **his Democratic counterpart, Chris Smith, who saw exactly zero fake news stories.**

But the problem goes beyond fake news. As Facebook's feeds prove, we live in a "post-truth" world, where the line between partisan spin and outright lies is practically indistinguishable now.

Fake News Fries

Ingredients

1 pkg fake fries of your choice. (Potato Broccoli, Sweet Potato and Kale, etc.)

- Ketchup
- Ranch Dressing
- BBQ Sauce

There are so many Fake Fries going around, you can't keep up!

Directions

Bake them at 425° for 20 minutes, flip them over once and continue baking for 10 minutes.

Short Version: Fry them with a light coating of olive oil or coconut oil, turning often.

FUN FACT

These are real articles from the "President Hillary Rodham Clinton" satirical website, with the major difference being that the Liberals know this is fake news and consider it to be comic relief.

Republicans probably don't know when they are getting 'Fake News' because they tend to be loyal to one news source - FOX... or "FAUX News," as liberals affectionately call it.

Democrats tend to listen to a variety of news sources, but appreciate a little comic-relief and prefer the President Clinton website type of fake news.

21

Trump Supporter Steak

"I could stand in the middle of 5th Avenue and shoot somebody and I still wouldn't lose any voters"

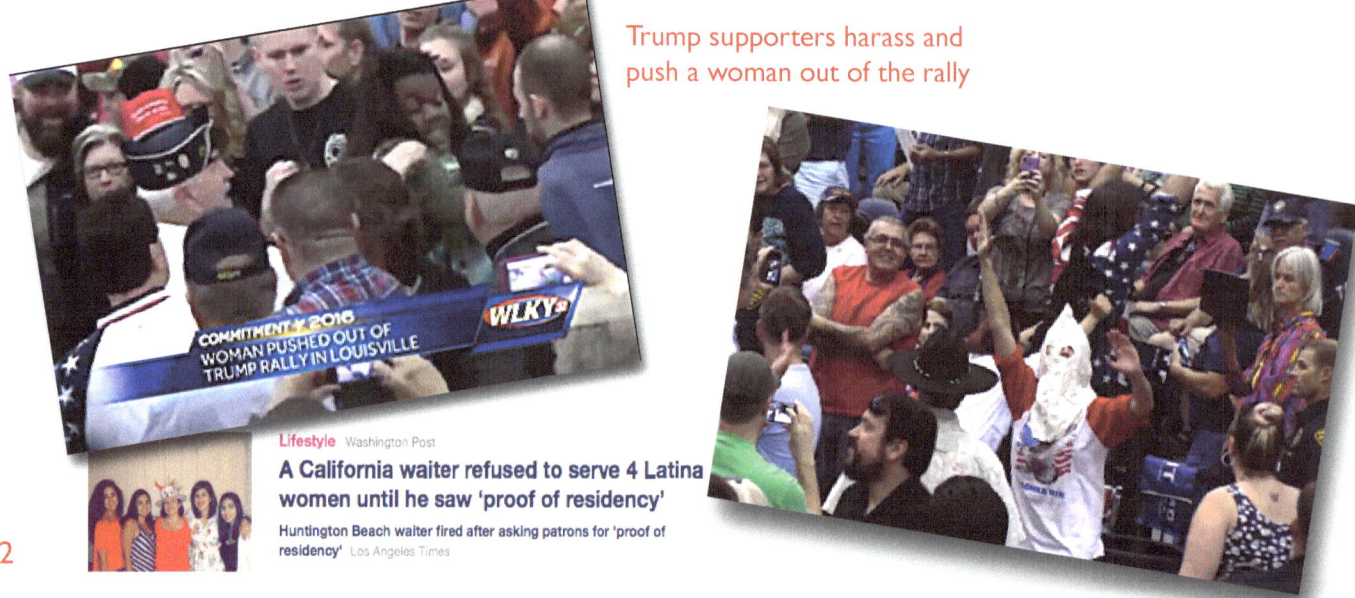

Trump supporters harass and push a woman out of the rally

22

Trump Supporter Steak

Ingredients

Trump Steak   Ketchup

Sizzle it up! Even if it comes out tough, Trump Supporters will love it anyway!

Directions

Grill it on a stick over an open fire - who needs conventions anyhow!?! Yeeeahhhh!
And don't tell us how to cook our own steak!

DON'T TREAD ON US!

FUN FACT

this is Russia

Politics USA Today

Anti-Trump billboard artist receives death threats

PHOENIX - Artist Karen Fiorito knew a backlash was bound to come. And it has. Commissioned by a downtown Phoenix ar...

A presidency based on ignorance, hate, exclusion, sexism, racism, greed and lawlessness....what could go wrong?

Republicans will support Trump even if/or because he lies repeatedly, seems to be racist, misogynistic, homophobic, has numerous lawsuits and sexual harassment cases pending and has unexplained ties to Russia AND no experience in a government office. He's an alpha winner! (to them)

Democrats don't think Trump is at all qualified for a US presidency because of the items (and many others) listed above and wish Republicans would wear their red hats at all times.

Crockpot Crow

Two weeks after Election Day -- as Donald Trump assembles his Cabinet -- votes in many states are still being counted. And the tally shows that Hillary Clinton's lead in the popular vote, with Michigan's 16 electoral votes still up for grab, continues to grow..

(Photo: Jewel Samad, AFP/Getty)

President-Elect Donald Trump has not taken kindly to the thousands of protesters flooding America's streets, and Fifth Avenue in particular, where daily demonstrations have snarled traffic throughout Midtown Manhattan and made living in Trump Tower a living hell. "Just had a very open and successful presidential election. Now professional protesters, incited by the media, are protesting," he fumed. The continued griping of the majority of Americans who did not vote for Trump has not gone over well with Trump's campaign manager, Kellyanne Conway, either, who dismissed protesters' grievances as the whining of entitled children.

"We're treating these adolescents and these millennials like **precious snowflakes,**" Conway said Wednesday night on Hannity, while discussing the trend of college professors canceling exams for upset students and giving them college credit for protesting.

"I'm just amazed by all the texts and e-mails I'm receiving," she said. **"What's the worst that can happen to these millennials?** That Donald Trump will make good on his promise to create 25 million new jobs?"

Of course, anti-Trump protesters likely have other concerns in mind. For non-white millennials, the "worst that can happen" begins with the recent rise of hate crimes against minorities in the wake of Trump's election, and escalates from there to the possibility of mass deportation of undocumented immigrants, a ban on all Muslims entering the country, the return of a federal Muslim registry, and nationwide stop-and-frisk.

Clinton supporters shocked, disappointed, and afraid - WRDW.com
www.wrdw.com/content/news/400515221.html
Nov 9, 2016 - NEW YORK (Gray DC) -- Hillary Clinton's supporters say they're disappointed, shocked, and afraid. Many of the voters who showed up to cheer ...

Crockpot Crow

Ingredients

- 1 or 2 Crows (plucked)
- 3 teaspoon olive oil
- 1 teaspoon Paprika
- 1 teaspoon ground garlic
- 1 teaspoon Cumin
- (it really doesn't matter what you put it. Nothing really matters anymore anyway.)

The worst, best tasting meal you'll ever have! When you have to eat Crow, it may as well be tasty!

Directions

Remove all or at least most of the feathers (substitute crow with chicken if preferred)
Put all liquid ingredients and seasonings in the crock pot. Mix. Add Crow (or Chicken)
Mix, toss and turn or stir occasionally.
Cook on LOW for 4-8 hrs
HIGH for 3-6 hrs, should be tender and completely fall apart like most HRC supporters at this point.

Note: I use de-boned, de-skinned, tenderloins when I have to eat crow. I find there is less to choke on that way.

Short Version: Pick up a rotisserie chicken from the deli department.
Eat small pieces and try not to choke, seriously.

The Electoral College Was Meant to Stop Men Like Trump From Being ...
https://www.theatlantic.com/politics/archive/2016/11/...electoral-college.../508310/

FUN FACT

Hillary Clinton's Final Popular Vote Lead Is 2.8 Million | Time
time.com/4608555/hillary-clinton-popular-vote-final/
Dec 20, 2016 - Hillary **Clinton's** lead in the **popular vote** of the 2016 presidential election was nearly three million votes more than Donald Trump.

Millions are petitioning the Electoral College to make Hillary Clinton...
www.businessinsider.com/can-the-electoral-college-make-hillary-clinton-president-ins...
Dec 6, 2016 - Over 4.9 million people signed a petition to encourage the **Electoral College** to make **Hillary** Clinton president instead, partly because she won ...

Republicans are over-joyed that they no longer have to be "politically correct" in public and look forward to "Making America Great Again" (though it is still unclear as to what time period they are referring to).

Democrats feel that the 'Deplorables' have won and brace themselves for gun-toting, racist, misogynist, non-regulated, fracking fanatics who believe in angels and war more than climate change and environmental protection.

Deplorable Duck Pie

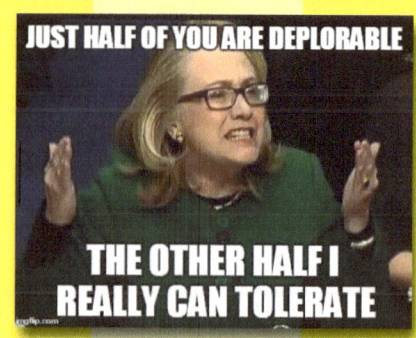

Basket of Deplorables

*"You know, to just be grossly generalistic, you could put half of Trump's supporters into what I call the **basket of deplorables**. The racist, sexist, homophobic, xenophobic, Islamophobic — you name it. And unfortunately there are people like that. And he has lifted them up."*

Donald Trump's Response
On September 10th, 2016 Republican presidential candidate Donald Trump published a press release denouncing Clinton's "deplorables" statement.

"Isn't it disgraceful that Hillary Clinton makes the worst mistake of the political season and instead of owning up to this grotesque attack on American voters, she tries to turn it around with a pathetic rehash of the words and insults used in her failing campaign? For the first time in a long while, her true feelings came out, showing bigotry and hatred for millions of Americans. How can she be President of our country when she has such contempt and disdain for so many great Americans? Hillary Clinton should be ashamed of herself, and this proves beyond a doubt that she is unfit and incapable to serve as President of the United States. I will be President for all of the people, and together we will Make America Great Again."

Clinton's Response

That day, Clinton released a statement expressing regret for saying "half" of Trump supporters were "deplorable," and accusing Trump of building his campaign "largely on prejudice and paranoia." Additionally, Clinton promised she "won't stop calling out bigotry and racist rhetoric in this campaign."

Deplorable Duck Pie

Ingredients

- 3 cups cubed Duck (or Turkey)
- 1 bag of diced Carrots & Peas
- 1 can Cream of Chicken Soup
- 1/2 cup Milk
- 1 pkg pie crust mix or Pillsbury biscuit canister

*Eat it up!
This Duck Pie is rich in Deplorableness.*

Directions

Heat oven to 425°F. Make pie crusts as directed on box for Two-Crust Pie, using 9-inch glass pie plate. In saucepan, cook the duck or turkey. Add the vegetables at medium heat approx. 2 minutes. Stir in the soup and milk, continue to heat for 5 minutes, then pour contents into a baking dish and gently spread the crust over the top.
Bake 30 to 40 minutes or until crust is golden brown.

Short Version: Buy Marie Calendar's Turkey Pot Pie and pop it in the microwave for 5 minutes.

You know, just to be grossly generalistic, you could put half of Trump's supporters into what I call the basket of deplorables. Right? The racist, sexist, homophobic, xenophobic, Islamaphobic—you name it. And unfortunately there are people like that. And he has lifted them up. He has given voice to their websites…He tweets and retweets their offensive hateful mean-spirited rhetoric.

Clinton went on to describe another "basket" of Trump supporters: "people who feel the government has let them down, the economy let them down, nobody cares about them." She stressed that "[t]hose are people we have to understand and empathize with as well."

FUN FACT

Republicans are over-joyed at the thought of having less government regulations for corporations and banks, no gun control, no handouts and big beautiful wall between the US and Mexico.

Democrats are split between Bernie and HRC but shudder to think what life in "Trump Land" would be like.

Millennial Meltdown

POLITICS 08/02/2016 01:38 pm ET | Updated Dec 29, 2016

How Third Party Voters And Non-Voters Could Shape The Election

Donald Trump and Hillary Clinton's unpopularity is causing voters to turn to alternatives.
By Samantha Neal [Huffington Post]

Hillary Clinton and Donald Trump may have enjoyed favorability bumps in the aftermath of their respective conventions, but the pair still has the highest disapproval ratings for presidential candidates since 1980. Many registered voters are consequently voting against the candidate from the opposing party rather than for their own, according to Pew Research.

FUN FACT

Unsurprisingly, there's been an increase in two groups that could influence the general election outcome: third-party backers and non-voters. Disaffected voters who refuse to support either Trump or Clinton are increasingly turning to third-party alternatives.

For those self-righteous proclaiming that they did not protest eight years ago, do you remember Rush Limbaugh stating on his nationally syndicated radio show, "We cannot let this president succeed"? Do you remember John Boehner and Mitch McConnell declaring they would block everything President Obama tried to do? How about the incessant lie that the president wasn't born in the U.S.? What about all of the right-wing internet articles declaring our president to be a Muslim terrorist sleeper agent? There were also the numerous articles that President Obama was un-American, and that he was intentionally weakening our military to the point that our Navy was weaker now than it was in 1917. The contempt even spread to the first lady, who was denigrated by Trump supporters.

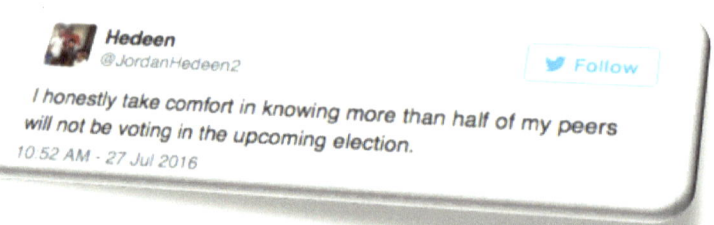

Millennial Meltdown

Ingredients

1 bag Corn Tortillas
1 cup Shredded Cheese
1 Avocado, sliced
1 cup Refried Beans
1 Jalapeño, sliced
1 Red Onion, minced
2 cloves Garlic, chopped
1 cup Cilantro, chopped
1 cup Salsa for dipping

Enjoy the variety of ingredients that come together for this raucous dish

Directions

Preheat your oven to 400°F
Arrange half of chips on a rimmed baking sheet lined with foil or a large cast iron skillet.
Top with half of each ingredients and repeat the layering with remaining chips and cheese, etc.
Bake in the oven until cheese has melted down like most Millenials - about 5 to 10 minutes.

46.6% didn't vote

25.6% voted for Hillary Clinton

25.5% voted for Donald Trump

1.7% voted for Gary Johnson

Approximate tallies

Clinton Won Millennial Vote But More Supported Third Party - The ...
https://www.theatlantic.com/education/archive/2016/11/dissecting-the...vote/507416/
Nov 11, 2016 - A national exit poll suggests more young adults in 2016 than in 2012 "supported a third-party candidate, did not **vote** for a presidential ...

FUN FACT

MILLENNIALS WOULD MAKE UP OVER 35% OF THE ELECTORATE IF THEY VOTED

Over **46%** of US Citizens **DIDN'T VOTE!**

As it turns out, approximately 48% of registered voters didn't vote. That is nearly half of the voters didn't vote (for HRC or Trump). So the current 'leader of the free world' won on less than 25% of registered American voters and did not win the popular vote.

Republicans believe the protesters are paid performers and have nothing better to do and/or are sore losers and should "Get Over It!"

Democrats feel saddened, sickened, disgusted and angry. They feel that any positive progress with equal rights, education, healthcare and green energy has been jerked backwards to some surreal land of ignorant, greedy and short-sighted, lawless thugs. (Note: I may be 'projecting' here, a bit...)

Protester Punch

USA

Germany

Some protest topics:
Travel Ban • Racism • Equal Pay • Women's Rights • Climate Change • GLBTQ Rights • Science March • EPA

The teachers will join women across America in drawing attention to "the enormous value that women of all backgrounds add to our socioeconomic system, while receiving lower wages and experiencing greater inequities, vulnerability to discrimination, sexual harassment and job insecurity," according to a statement by the campaigners who are organising the demonstration.

"Women across the nation, as well as men, will be participating in a one-day demonstration to recognise the value of women," it said. "As part of this demonstration, many will be staying home from work."

So many protests - So little time...

Protest marches in DC were also carried out in nearly every major city (on a smaller scale). Protesters even felt strongly enough to gather and march in international cities. The right to protest is a big part of the American culture...and the constitution.

England

France

Protester Punch

Ingredients

1 extra large bottle of Rum
1 Bottle Grenadine
1 Quart Tonic Water
1 Quart Orange Juice

Garnish with Maraschino Cherries, Orange Slices and/or more rum

Enjoy the punch and kick of the Protester Punch, it's sure to knock you on your butt!

Directions

Mix it all together, pour over ice, garnish with fruit and drink as necessary. Be sure to share!

Republicans don't care about the national and international protests against Trump. They think the Democrats and "Libtards" should, "Get Over It!"

Democrats continue to 'RESIST' and protest the Trump agenda of what they see as being racist, sexist, anti-education, anti-community, anti-environmental and war-starting.

Black Rye Matters

blacklivesmatter.com

Black Lives Matter is an ideological and political intervention in a world where Black lives are systematically and intentionally targeted for demise. It is an affirmation of Black folks' contributions to this society, our humanity, and our resilience in the face of deadly oppression.

White people make up roughly 62 percent of the U.S. population but only about 49 percent of those who are killed by police officers. African Americans, however, account for 24 percent of those fatally shot and killed by the police despite being just 13 percent of the U.S. population. As The Post noted in a new analysis published last week, that means black Americans are 2.5 times as likely as white Americans to be shot and killed by police officers.
U.S. police officers have shot and killed the exact same number of unarmed white people as they have unarmed black people: 50 each. But because the white population is approximately five times as great as the black population, that means unarmed black Americans were five times as likely as unarmed white Americans to be shot and killed by a police officer.

And, when considering shootings confined within a single race, a black person shot and killed by police is more likely to have been unarmed than a white person. About 13 percent of all black people who have been fatally shot by police since January 2015 were unarmed, compared with 7 percent of all white people.

A 2015 study by a University of California at Davis researcher concluded there was "no relationship" between crime rates by race and racial bias in police killings. A report released last week by the Center for Policing Equity, which reviewed arrest and use-of-force data from 12 police departments, concluded that black residents were more often targeted for use of police force than white residents, even when adjusting for whether the person was a violent criminal.

One of the worst issues of American history – Civilians gunned down in the street by the law enforcement that is meant to 'serve and protect' them. You may take it a lot more seriously if it happened to you or a love one.

Black Rye Matters

Ingredients

- 1 Loaf Black Rye Bread
- 1 Cup shredded Parmesan Cheese
- 3 Cloves Garlic diced, or 2 tsp minced Garlic or sprinkle Garlic Power
- 4 tbsp Olive Oil or Coconut Oil
- Oregano

Slice it up however you like, it will still be the same

Directions

Preheat Oven to 350°
Lay tin foil over flat cookie sheet.
Spread Olive Oil, Coconut Oil or butter over every slice of Rye (topside and bottom)
Spread minced garlic (or garlic powder) over the slices.
Sprinkle Parmesan cheese and oregano.
Add salt and pepper to taste.
Bake for 10 minutes or whatever...keep an eye on it.

> Black Americans are **2.5 times** as likely as white Americans to be stopped, shot and killed by police officers.

Multiple NYPD cops choke a peaceful...
YouTube - 1280 × 720 - Search by image
Multiple NYPD cops choke a peaceful man (Eric Garner) to death WATCH

HEADLINE JAN 17, 2017
Cleveland: Officers to Face Disciplinary Charges in Tamir Rice Death

U.S. Marie Claire
Jeff Sessions Deals a Blow to Black Lives Matter
Updating Live: Tracking Donald Trump's First 100 Days in Office Marie Claire

Republican response is "All Lives Matter." Generally they have no (or very little) idea what the movement is about and don't want to hear about it.

Democrats recognize the origins of the problem and proposed that law enforcement officers wear body-cameras and gain more training, as a first step.

Pipeline Pasta

"WATER IS LIFE"

Water protectors from the Oceti Sakowin camp, the main protest camp at Standing Rock, have just issued an urgent message in the form of a short video. According to the two-minute clip, the camp has been surrounded by "heavily militarized law enforcement."

The news follows reports in early February that—following a Trump executive order—Army secretary Jack Speer had ordered the Army Corps of Engineers to allow construction of the Dakota Access Pipeline to resume under the stretch of the Missouri River adjacent to the Standing Rock Sioux reservation.

Over the course of months-long, ongoing protest efforts at Standing Rock, law enforcement have already used force against protesters several times, including water cannons, tear gas, and concussion grenades "In the history of colonization, they've always given us two options," explains a protester in the video, "Give up our land or go to jail." Narrated and produced by women at the camp, the video is a call to actions for journalists and allies alike to come lend support:

"Protectors. Media. Get here by Feb. 21. The police have surrounded Oceti Sakowin Camp.

Stand with us in peace and prayer to protect the water and treaty rights. We are unarmed. Mni Wiconi. Water is life."

Sam Levin in Cannon Ball, North Dakota • Wednesday 8 February 2017 18.02 EST

"I came back to stand for our people," Rowland said, as he prepared a large stew inside his family's wooden hut. Around him, young children took shelter from sub-zero temperatures outside.
Rowland – who arrived at Standing Rock last August, but went home in January – is one of a number of Native Americans who rushed back this week to the camps in Cannon Ball, North Dakota, to fight the $3.7bn pipeline. The activists, who call themselves "water protectors", are now planning demonstrations, prayer walks and other resistance efforts a day after the US army corps of engineers announced it was approving the final phase of construction of the pipeline.

> *On Wednesday, the army corps formally granted Dakota Access the final permit it requires to drill under the Missouri river. "We plan to begin drilling immediately," a spokeswoman for the company said.*

Pipeline Pasta

Ingredients

- 1 bag Rigatoni
- 1 lb Ground Beef
- 3 tablespoons Olive Oil
- 1 Onion, chopped
- 1 Green Bell Pepper
- 1 tsp Italian Seasoning
- 1 Cayenne Pepper
- 1 can Tomato Sauce
- 1 can Diced Tomatoes
- 1/4 cup Tomato Paste
- 1 tablespoon Sugar or Honey
- Parmesan Cheese to taste

Use extra sauce to make sure all of that goopey goodness flows through and leaks out everywhere

Directions

Boil pasta until tender, about 12 minutes then strain and set aside.
In large pot over medium heat oil. Add onion and bell pepper and cook, stirring occasionally, until soft, about 5 minutes. Stir in ground beef and cook, stirring and breaking up meat chunks with a spoon. Cook until meat is done, about 7 minutes until no longer pink. Add spaghetti sauce, honey and spices. Add pasta. Mix well. Sprinkle with Parmesan cheese

FUN FACT

Added bonus for Republicans: (devastating for Democrats)
The Trump Administration seeks to repeal the current corporate regulations that help to protect workers and the environment. AND appoints a person who wants to dismantle the EPA (Environmental Protection Agency) as the head of the EPA.

FUN FACT

Republicans chant, "Drill Baby Drill!" They want to focus on oil fracking and coal mining.

Democrats want to protect the environment and focus on 'Green Energy' production.

Pigs-In-A-Blanket

'To Serve and Protect'...

Contrary to some police doctrines, some police officers told Balko that dressing officers in military garb does not scare protesters into order. Instead, it actually ramps up the feeling of imminent conflict. For example, Jerry Wilson, who took over as police chief of Washington D.C. shortly after the riots in that city in the wake of Martin Luther King, Jr.'s assassination, believed that appearing as a hostile, military force actually invited conflict.

"That didn't mean Wilson didn't prepare," Balko wrote. "[B]ut he put his riot control teams in buses, then parked the buses close by, but out of sight of protesters. Appearances were important. In general, instead of the usual brute force and reactionary policing that tended to pit cops against citizens—both criminal and otherwise—Wilson believed that cops were more effective when they were welcomed and respected in the neighborhoods they patrolled."

Balko notes that violence and riots declined in Washington during Wilson's tenure. There was a completely different response in Ferguson and Berkeley, where police took an aggressive stance similar to what we saw in Seattle during the G-8 protests in 1999 or in New York during the height of Occupy Wall Street. Police came out in riot gear, looking like soldiers.

Norm Stamper, who was Seattle's police chief in 1999, regrets his decision to forcefully oppose the protesters.

"We gassed fellow Americans engaging in civil disobedience," Stamper told Balko.
"We set a number of precedents, most of them bad. And police departments across the country learned all the wrong lessons from us. That's disheartening. So disheartening. I mean, you look at what happened to those Occupy protesters at U.C. Davis, where the cop just sprays them down like he's watering a bed of flowers, and I think that we played a part in making that sort of thing so common—so easy to do now. It's beyond cringe-worthy. I wish to hell my career had ended on a happier note."

FUN FACT

Pigs-In-A-Blanket

Ingredients

1 Package of Hot Dogs
Pillsbury Crescent Roll
or pie crust mix

Mustard gas Sauce
Spicy BBQ Sauce
Relish

Enjoy these little delights nice and hot - be sure to give 'em a little 'taze' if necessary

Directions

Cut dough into triangle shapes or thin (1/2 inch) strips.
Put the hotdog on the widest side of the triangle and roll the hotdog and dough. Press to bind the dough in place. Place the pigs in a blanket on cookie sheet (not touching each other and bake at 350° for 20 minutes or until the dough is golden. and flaky.

"There is nobody better than a good cop. There is nobody worse than a bad cop."

FUN FACT

Thorough investigations, heavy fines and jail time for all of those operating above the law, should be standard procedure.
Law Enforcement MUST BE HELD ACCOUNTABLE for violations against citizens. Higher diversity ratios within the force, along with surveillance camera & audio should also be standard procedure.

Don't Lose Sight of the Good Cops

Anthony Hatcher | Posted 05.22.2016 | Crime

Read More: Ferguson, Freddie Gray, New York Police Department, Nyclu, Good Cops, Crime News

Recent events in Baltimore, Ferguson, New York or wherever an unarmed black man has died in police custody remind me of something I learned long ago when I was on the police beat: There is nobody better than a good cop. There is nobody worse than a bad cop.

Republicans think cops wont stop you, if you are not doing anything wrong and fatally shooting an unarmed person is OK if the officers was scared.

Democrats believe there is a problem with police brutality cases (especially towards people of color) but realize the difficulties of law enforcement. No one should be allowed to operate above the law.

Winning Wild Rice Soup

"We must reclaim our country's destiny," said Trump. "We're going to dream of things for our country, of beautiful things, of successful things once again."

"We are gonna win, win, win!

We're going to win with military, we're going to win at the borders, we're going to win with trade, we're going to win at everything.

"Get rid of Obamacare!"

And some of you are friends and you're going to call, and you're going to say,
Mr. President, please, we can't take it anymore, we can't win anymore like this, Mr. President, you're driving us crazy, you're winning too much, please Mr. President, not so much, and I'm going to say I'm sorry, we're going to keep winning because we are going to make America great again."

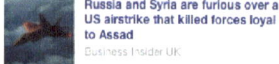

...um, was that a little bit creepy, or is it just me...

"The wall is ahead of schedule!"

March 2017

Donald J. Trump @realDonaldTrump · Jun 11
Great numbers on the economy. All of our work, including the passage of many bills & regulation killing Executive Orders, now kicking in!

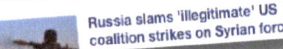

Winning Wild Rice Soup

Ingredients

- 1 can of Cream of Chicken (celery, mushroom, potato or onion wins well too)
- 1 cup Wild Rice (cooked)
- 1 teaspoon Garlic powder
- 1 teaspoon Turmeric

When you are tired of winning, recharge with Winning Wild Rice soup!

Directions

So tired of winning...can't do the long version of the recipe. Just use the "Short Version."

Short Version:
Get a package of pre-made wild rice in a pouch and a can of Cream of Chicken.
Mix 'em all together in a saucepan with medium heat.
Add some seasonings. - enjoy all the winning!

Republicans are happy to be winning again! Corporate regulations rolled back, tax breaks for the wealthy, building a wall that will cost the tax payers only 1.5 billion to keep out Mexicans that are "stealing our jobs." Huge funding cuts for Medicaid, the disabled, school lunch programs, EPA - gone! And Bombing - showed his bravado in foreign affairs and the possibility of war. ...so much winning!

Democrats don't feel that anyone is winning under the Trump Administration, except for the corporations and the already wealthy 1%ers. But maybe, just maybe, Trump will grow as a person and it will all be OK.

Swampwater Martini

*Trump supporters were probably hoping that the president-elect's Cabinet choices would reflect his **drain the swamp** mantra,*

but it's becoming clear that Trump's version of that is the opposite of what he promised. His version of draining the swamp was actually to fill it with people who spread conspiracy theories, bankers, CEOs, retired generals, politicians, and billionaires. Basically, we are looking at a bunch of people who are so deep in the swamp they'd need a periscope to see the sun.

Upon closer inspection, Trump actually does appear to be draining something: experience. An alarming number of Trump's picks for Cabinet or other high-level agency positions possess a striking dearth of relevant qualifications for the fields in which they will be working. It's set to be a veritable parade of people who don't know what they're doing.

"and will not be questioned!"

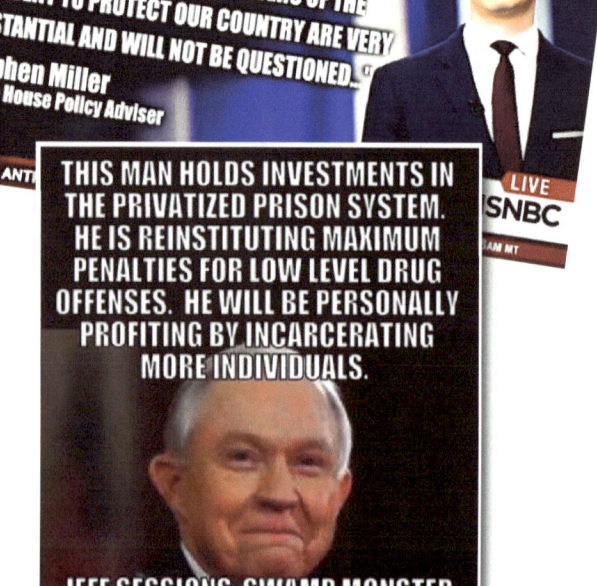

Swampwater Martini

Ingredients

Lots of Gin

Jars of Green Olives
Twigs

Drain that Swampwater right into your glass for the best dern Dirty Martini ever!

Directions

1. Git 'yer self a big ol bucket (toss out the tadpoles first)
2. Pour in all them bottles of gin (or your favorite moonshine)
3. Pour in all them jars of olives and the juice.
4. Give that bucket a big ol swish around.
5. Find yerself a nice little stick (peel off the bark) and harpoon a few of them olives.
6. Dip yer fancy Martini glass right in there and git you some!
7. Injoy!

Republicans are glad Trump is getting rid of all the politicians and replacing them with KKK/Breitbart associates, Russian connections and Wall Street bankers.

Democrats are nauseous and are rolling their eyes while reaching for a Swampwater Martini. (so much for wishful thinking...)

Mediterranean Mix-Up

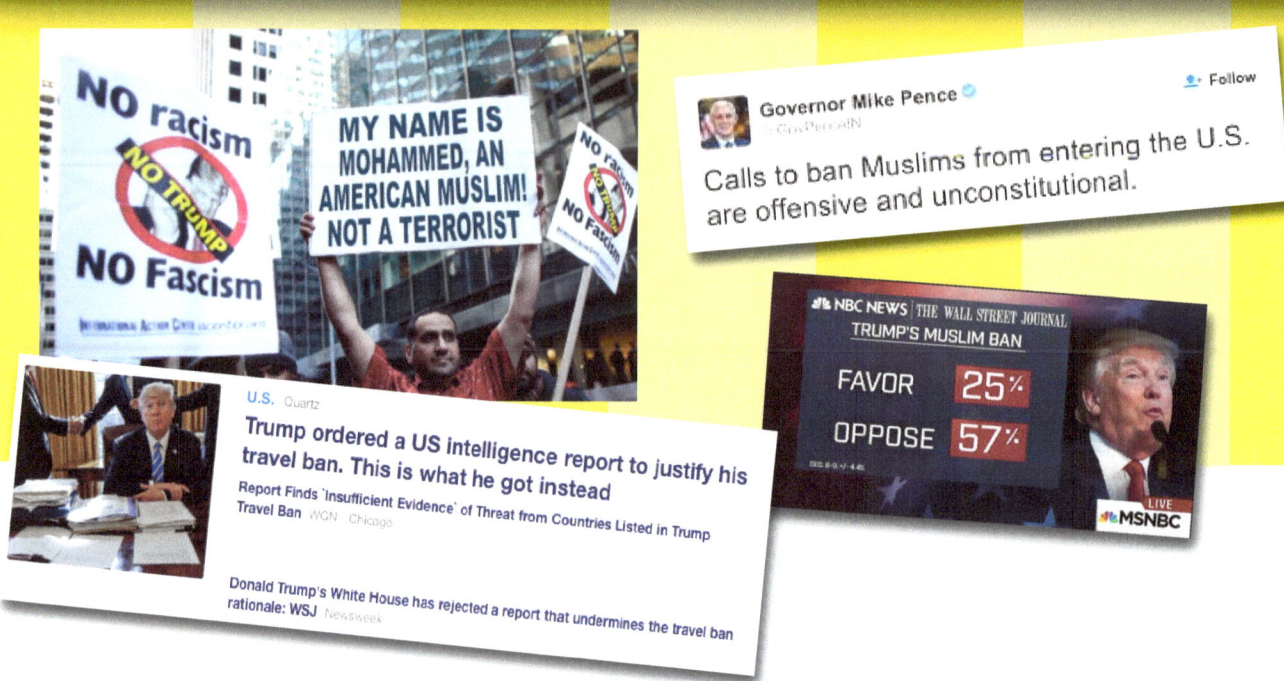

TSA and White House Officials were uninformed and unprepared for the ban.

Fatemeh and her family received an all-clear to enter the US for critical surgery, N.Y. Gov. Andrew Cuomo announced Friday.

The family was going to fly to Portland, Oregon, where they have relatives, so Fatemeh could get the treatment she needs. They flew to Dubai, but when they arrived, they were rerouted back to Iran and told to reapply for a US visa in 90 days. *Many state and federal officials have intervened on behalf of the family*, a Washington, D.C.-based immigration attorney working on the case, Amber Murray told CNN.

42

Mediterranean Mix-Up

Ingredients

- 1 Pkg Pasta (angel hair, fettuccine, spaghetti whatever)
- 1 Red Bell Pepper
- 1 Yellow Bell Pepper
- 1 Green Bell Pepper
- 1 Red Onion
- 6 Chicken Tenderloins
- 1/4 Diced Olives
- 1 Cup Feta Cheese (Crumbles)
- 1/4 Cup Olive Oil
- Fresh Parsley, chopped
- Crushed Red Pepper
- Ground Black Pepper
- Shredded Parmesan Cheese

An interesting blend of Mediterranean flavor rolls out so smoothly

Directions

Mix everything up and see how it turns out. -
No, don't do that. Let's think about this for a minute...
Bring 6 cups of water to a boil. Add the pasta. Add a teaspoon of oil to keep pasta from sticking together. Sprinkle some oregano in the water (because it smells nice). Reduce heat to medium and continue to boil until tender, about 15 minutes. Drain the pasta and leave it in the strainer.
Use your same pot to cook the chicken (less dishes). Use medium heat and a little olive oil. Cook the chicken thoroughly, add spices. Remove the chicken when cooked and cut into small pieces while your previously cut into strips bell peppers and onions are now cooking in that same pan. What? A little confusing? Don't worry about it. Everything is going along just fine.

After the pasta, chicken, peppers and onion are all chopped and cooked, reunite them in that original pot and mix them together. Add the olive oil and fresh parsley, sage, crushed red pepper. Gently mix in the feta cheese and set on low heat. Serve with shredded Parmesan cheese and fresh ground Pepper.

Republicans like the ban and see it as a step towards "Making America Great Again."

Democrats see the ban as unconstitutional. They see it as discriminatory - fueling hate and possible retaliation. But regardless of your position, they believe it was not done in a thought-out way.

Fiesta Border Casserole

"Mexico will not pay for your f*cking wall!"
~Vicente Fox

"The wall is ahead of schedule!"

"The administration is asking the American taxpayer to cover the cost of a wall — unneeded, ineffective, absurdly expensive — that Mexico was supposed to pay for, and he is cutting programs vital to the middle class to get that done," said Senate Minority Leader Chuck Schumer, D-N.Y. "Build the wall or repair or build a bridge or tunnel or road in your community? What's the choice?"

FUN FACT

Fiesta Border Casserole

Ingredients

- 1 pound lean Ground Beef
- 2 cups Salsa
- 1 can Chili Beans, drained
- 3 cups Tortilla Chips
- 2 cups Sour Cream
- 1/2 cup Green Onion, diced
- 1/2 cup Tomato, diced
- 2 cups Shredded Cheddar Cheese

Directions

Be sure to install the tortilla strip wall right down the middle, so we know who's side you're on

Heat oven to 350°F. In 10-inch skillet, cook beef over medium heat 8 to 10 minutes, stirring occasionally, until brown; drain. Stir in beans and 1 cup salsa. Heat to boiling, stirring occasionally. In ungreased 2-quart casserole, place broken tortilla chips. Top with beef mixture. Sprinkle with onions, tomato and cheese. Bake uncovered 20 to 30 minutes or until hot and aggravated. Arrange tortilla chips straight down the middle of casserole.
Serve with lettuce and additional salsa.

Republicans are thrilled to have "illegals" rounded up and deported so they can feel safe again and get their jobs back. And extra glad that Mexico will pay for the wall like Trump promised.

Democrats believe there should be a thorough immigration process, but don't see this issue as a major threat to their existence.

Humble Hummingbird Cake

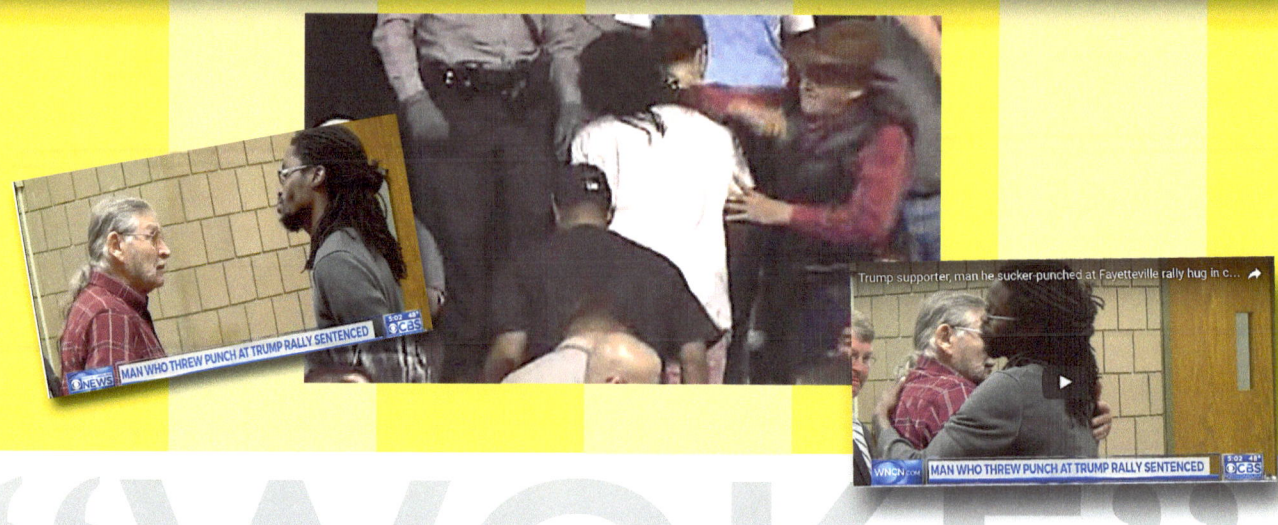

"WOKE"

Meanwhile...

"You and me, we're going to heal our country."

Last March, a viral video caught the moment when John Franklin McGraw sucker punched Rakeem Jones while the latter was being escorted out of a Donald Trump rally in Fayetteville, North Carolina. McGraw was charged with assault and battery, making him the first person to face serious fines and possible jail time for inciting violence against a protester at a Trump rally. A charge of communicating threats was later added when comments McGraw made about enjoying the punch and possibly having to kill Jones were aired on Inside Edition.

Most would assume McGraw and Jones' demeanor towards one another wouldn't have changed much during the former's sentencing on Wednesday. However, as video captured by CBS affiliate WNCN shows, the two men had come to an understanding — so much that they faced one another, shook hands, and hugged it out. "We're caught up in a political mess today," said McGraw, adding: "You and me, we're going to heal our country."

FUN FACT

Side Dish: If you secretly or openly feel that you have now been given a license to behave badly towards others, make no mistake about it -
YOU ARE *the problem.*

Humble Hummingbird Cake

Ingredients

1 package Spice Cake Mix with pudding (2 layer size) add ingredients according to pkg
1 cup mashed ripe Banana
1 teaspoon Vanilla extract
1 teaspoon Cinnamon
1 cup chopped Pecans, toasted
1 Cream Cheese frosting (8oz)

Be humble and enjoy this Humble Hummingbird Cake - so nice and sweet

Directions

Preheat oven to 350 degrees. Grease and flour a 12 cup bundt pan.
Mix on low speed for 1 minute the cake mix, pineapple and juice, bananas, water, oil, eggs, vanilla and cinnamon. Stop mixer and scrape down, then mix at medium speed for 2 minutes more. Stir in by hand the cherries and 1/2 cup nuts. Batter will be thick and fruit well blended. Pour into bundt pan. Bake on middle rack for 50-60 minutes. Cake will be golden and spring back when touched. Cool in pan for 20 minutes then invert and cool completely.

Make the cream cheese frosting. Mix the cream cheese and butter on low 30 seconds. Add the sugar, slowly still at low speed until well blended. Add vanilla, increase to medium and beat 1 minute. Frost cooled cake and sprinkle with the remaining 1/2 cup pecans.

Short Version: Pick up a spice coffee cake at the bakery - It's easy for them, they do it all the time.

en·ti·tle·ment
/inˈtīdlmənt,enˈtīdlmənt/

noun

the belief that one is inherently deserving of privileges or special treatment.
"no wonder your kids have a sense of entitlement"

Republicans may not know about this, or may not want to know about this, or may have considered it to be "fake news."

Democrats are amazed at this evolution of social understanding though they notice the lack of appropriate punishment for the physical assault and death treat dealt by 70 Year Old John McGraw and the fact that the victim was the one handcuffed and escorted out by 'law enforcement'

Twitter Tortellini

Personal Superlatives

1. "My I.Q. is one of the highest - and you all know it!"
2. "I will be the best by far in fighting terror"
3. "I will be the greatest job-producing president in American history"
4. "I am the BEST builder, just look at what I've built"
5. "I am the best builder but if that were my building with the crane mishap…"
6. "I am attracting the biggest crowds, by far, and the best poll numbers, also by far."

Donald J. Trump @realDonaldTrump

Watched low rated @Morning_Joe for first time in long time. FAKE NEWS. He called me to stop a National Enquirer article. I said no! Bad show

Joe Scarborough @JoeNBC

Yet another lie. I have texts from your top aides and phone records. Also, those records show I haven't spoken with you in many months.

Donald J. Trump @realDonaldTrump

Sorry losers and haters, but my I.Q. is one of the highest -and you all know it! Please don't feel so stupid or insecure, it's not your fault
7:37 PM - 8 May 2013

Donald J. Trump @realDonaldTrump

The concept of global warming was created by and for the Chinese in order to make U.S. manufacturing non-competitive.
12:15 PM - 6 Nov 2012

Donald J. Trump @realDonaldTrump

An 'extremely credible source' has called my office and told me that @BarackObama's birth certificate is a fraud.
2:23 PM - 6 Aug 2012

Twitter Tortellini

Ingredients

1 pkg Three Cheese Tortellini
1 cup Pesto
2 Tbsp butter or Coconut oil
2 Garlic Cloves (chopped)
1/2 cup Parmesan cheese

2 Tbsp Sour Cream
1/2 cup Mozzarella cheese
1/2 cup Fresh chopped
Salt and Cracked Black pepper
Sage leaves

Some people just can't get enough of this Twitter Tortellini.

Directions

Cook tortellini in a large pot with some salted water, according to the package. Drain and set aside.
In a small sauce pot, melt butter over medium heat and add pressed garlic.
Saute until fragrant (just a few seconds) and slowly add heavy cream WHILE whisking. Heat through on medium heat, keep stirring slowly.
Add sour cream, Parmesan cheeses, salt and pepper. Keep cooking on medium-low heat for about 5-7 minutes, stirring often, until all smooth.

In the pot where you cooked the tortellini, add pesto and mix well. Add Alfredo sauce and Mozzarella cheese. Mix well and serve. Top each plate with some fresh grated Parmesan cheese.

Donald J. Trump @realDonaldTrump   [Follow]
.@NBCNews is bad but Saturday Night Live is the worst of NBC. Not funny, cast is terrible, always a complete hit job. Really bad television!
3:46 PM · 15 Jan 2017

Donald J. Trump @realDonaldTrump · Apr 23
New polls out today are very good considering that much of the media is FAKE and almost always negative. Would still beat Hillary in .....

Donald J. Trump @realDonaldTrump · May 5
Of course the Australians have better healthcare than we do --everybody does. ObamaCare is dead! But our healthcare will soon be great.

FUN FACT

Australia has the same type of healthcare system that Obamacare was modeled after.

Republicans like hearing directly from "The Donald." They feel more connected and better informed, whether they are getting "alternative facts" or not.

Democrats find the tweets to be reckless and/or dangerous in some cases or entertaining, at best.

Alternative Swedish Meatballs

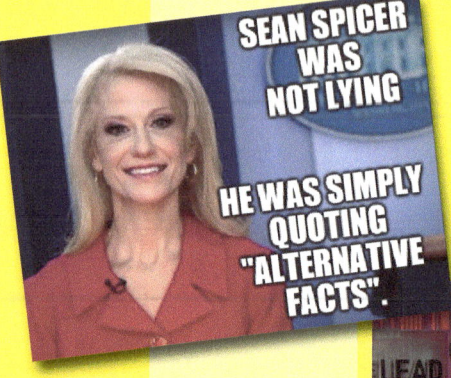

"Alternative Facts" have made it impossible to have any meaningful conversations and have frustrated many a journalist and news anchors.

But the problem goes beyond fake news. As Facebook's feeds prove, we live in a "post-truth" world, where the line between partisan spin and outright lies is practically indistinguishable.

Kellyanne Conway Said "Bowling Green Massacre" in Another Interview
www.cosmopolitan.com/politics/.../kellyanne-conway-bowling-green-massacre-repeat... ▼
Feb 6, 2017 - That MSNBC interview was not the first time Kellyanne Conway mentioned the nonexistent "Bowling Green Massacre." She also used the ...

Politics Newsweek
Robert Reich: How Trump lies about his many lies
Earlier this year, The Wall Street Journal's editor-in-chief insisted that The Wall Street Journal wouldn't label Donald...

Politics The Week
Fact-checkers had a field day with President Trump's address to Congress
Reacting to President Trump's address to Congress Yahoo News Video

President Trump Addresses Congress: 7 Supremely Uncomfortable Moments TVLine.com

The readers' editor on exposing fake news and lies | Stephen Pritchard
Checking facts is more important than ever as fake news becomes the refuge of the angry

Politics Newsweek
No, Trump Has Not Created 600,000 Jobs Since Becoming President
Trump Will Lift the Federal Hiring Freeze but Many Jobs Likely to Remain Unfilled Fortune

In an interview on NBC's "Meet the Press," host Chuck Todd pressed Trump senior adviser **Kellyanne Conway** about why the White House on Saturday had sent Spicer to the briefing podium for the first time to claim that "this was the largest audience to ever witness an inauguration, period." "You're saying it's a falsehood. Jan 23, 2017

Conway: Trump White House offered 'alternative facts' on crowd size ...
www.cnn.com/2017/01/22/politics/kellyanne-conway-alternative-facts/

Alternative Swedish Meatballs

Ingredients

- 1 Pkg of Vegetarian Meatballs
- 1 jar Vegetarian Brown Gravy
- 4 cups of Mashed Potatoes
- 3 tablespoons Olive Oil
- 3 Tablespoons fresh Parsley
- Salt
- Pepper

Try Alternative Swedish Meatballs for when facts just aren't palatable

Directions

Defrost the fake (correction: I mean "Alternative") meatballs and set aside. Mix up the fake potatoes as directed on the package. Heat the fake brown gravy. Add the meatballs to the gravy. Dish out the fake mashed potatoes topped with the ...oh yeah... "Alternative Meatballs"

FBI's Comey: 'I have no information' to support Trump's wiretapping tweets

CNBC · 4 hours ago

Republicans are OK with "Alternative Facts." Many are religious and are used to a "faith-based" ideology. They are fiercely loyal to the Republican party no matter what.

Democrats generally tune-in to several news feeds NPR, BBC, PBS, CNN, NYT, WSJ, MSN, (and even Fox, albeit for entertainment purposes) and have been aware of "alternative facts" largely spun from conservative news outlets.

Hypocrisy Hamburg Heaven

Trump inherited his $$ and network of wealthy contacts. He has stiffed contractors out of their pay and hired illegal immigrants on a regular basis. Skipped out of active duty because of a bone spur but calls US solders weak for suffering from PTSD.

Politics Business Insider
Sean Spicer angrily defends Trump's wiretap claims in wild, contentious press...
White House repeats claim British spy agency monitored Trump AFP

FUN FACT

Barack Obama took 28 vacation trips lasting 217 days through nearly eight years in office (that count came as of fall 2016), while George W. Bush took 88 trips lasting 533 days. Guess which one drew more Republican ire, and specifically the ire of one Donald J. Trump? And guess who is heading off for a little Florida vacation this weekend again?

229 Republicans Voted Last Night to Prevent You from Ever Seeing Donald Trump's Tax Returns

marieclaire Associated Press, Marie Claire

From Marie Claire
House Republicans have blocked an attempt by Democrats to force President Donald Trump to release his tax returns to Congress.

THAT FACE YOU MAKE WHEN "PRES. CROTCH-GRABBER" WISHES WOMEN A HAPPY INTERNATIONAL WOMEN'S DAY

Politics CNN
Trump's estates are costing taxpayers millions
President Trump's large real estate is costing US taxpayers money, but one of the more underused presidential propertie

FUN FACT

In Under 3 Months, Trump Spent Almost Double Obama's Annual Travel Budget
This marked the seventh weekend that President Trump spent at what he has come to call the "Winter White House" since taking office on Jan. 20. It is e...
SLATE.COM

DON'T TRUMP ON ME

Tomi Lahren's nightly show pulled for a week after her abortion comments

POLITICS NATIONAL POLITICS
"I'm pro-choice," says Tomi Lahren: "Stay out of my guns, and you can stay out of my body"
Washington Post 5 hours ago

Tomi Lahren Has Reportedly Been Suspended From Her Show After ...
https://www.buzzfeed.com/stephaniemcneal/tomi-lahren-pro-choice ▼
20 hours ago - Conservative talk show host **Tomi Lahren** has reportedly been suspended from her show on The Blaze, after her recent admission she supports ...

"Real women don't protest"
`Tomi Lahren`
...unless of course something shatters their snow-globe world. Right Tammi? "Shit happens. Get over it!"
(as she would say)

Trump's hidden tax returns take on new significance | MSNBC
www.msnbc.com/rachel-maddow.../trumps-hidden-tax-returns-take-new-significance ▼
Jul 26, 2016 - Donald **Trump** has a responsibility to release his **tax** returns anyway, but the controversy with Russia add urgency to the equation.

Hypocrisy Hamburg Heaven

Ingredients

1 1/2 pounds Ground Beef
1 Egg
1 pkg Onion Soup Mix, dry
1 cup Milk
1 cup dried bread crumbs
salt and pepper to taste

2 tablespoons Brown Sugar
1/3 cup Ketchup or
BBQ Sauce

Dig into this heaping dish of Hypocrisy Hamburg Heaven - there is plenty to go around!

Directions

Preheat oven to 350 degrees F (175 degrees C).
In a large bowl, combine the beef, egg, onion, milk and bread OR cracker crumbs. Season with salt and pepper to taste and place in a lightly greased 5x9 inch loaf pan, OR form into a loaf and place in a lightly greased 9x13 inch baking dish.
In a separate small bowl, combine the brown sugar and ketchup or BBQ sauce.
Mix well and pour over the meatloaf.
Bake at 350 degrees for 1 hour.

*"Birth certificate?
How 'bout them tax returns..."*

World The Huffington Post
Majority Of Republicans Said 'No' When Obama Wanted To Launch A Strike On Syria
Trump supporters against military action in Syria? Fox Business Videos

MAR-A-LAGO
Donald Trump Should Chip In for His Expensive Mar-a-Lago Golf Getaways
Dear Mr. President, I'm writing with a modest proposal. You've got a lot on your plate. Heal...

Republican don't seem to notice and/or care about the Trump Campaign's and Administration's hypocritical behavior.

Democrats are astounded by the many incidents of hypocrisy.

Ironic Seafood Salad

Greg 21 minutes ago

"Before being elected President, Mr. Trump was one of the most successful businessmen in the world". Is this a joke? He inherited his daddy's money, had his daddy co-sign his business deals, and has gone bankrupt . How is that success? i respect real success stories.

Note: A sarcastic parody tweet, but still ironic

 Donald Trump
Yesterday at 21:22

My grandparents didn't come to America all the way from Germany just to see it get taken over by immigrants. Not on my watch.

U.S. International Business Times

Trump supporter's undocumented Mexican husband deported

The Husband Of A "Mislead" Trump Supporter Has Been Deported Back To Mexico Vibe

Lawmakers: Trump should seek war-making authority

Donald Trump insisted four years ago that then-President Barack Obama needed congressional...

War Powers Resolution option »

 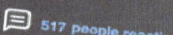 517 people reacting

 Donald J. Trump @realDonaldTrump · Feb 7
It is a disgrace that my full Cabinet is still not in place, the longest such delay in the history of our country. Obstruction by Democrats!

Politics Quartz

A well-timed Oval Office photo perfectly illustrates Trump's revelation that being president is hard

No one thought it would be easy, except, apparently Donald Trump. Nearing his 100th day in office, the US president sat down for an interview with Reuters on Thursday (Apr. 27) and...

 Trump says being president is harder than he expected
BostonGlobe.com

 How President Trump forced late-night TV to evolve
Vox.com

Business International Business Times UK

Mexican cement company says it will 'gladly' provide materials for construction ...

LafargeHolcim "ideally positioned" to benefit from Trump's trillion-dollar infrastructure plan: CEO CNBC

Ironic Seafood Salad

Ingredients

3 stalks Celery thinly sliced
3 cloves Garlic chopped
Juice of 1 Lemon
8 oz shredded Carrots
3/4 pound small Shrimp, peeled
1/2 pound Sea Scallops, halved
1 small Avocado
2 Romaine Lettuce Hearts
2 cups Croutons
1 tablespoon Mayonnaise
1 tablespoon Olive Oil

You will enjoy this uniquely satisfying, iron-rich dish.

Directions

Combine the quartered celery, smashed garlic, half of the lemon juice, 10 cups water, and salt and pepper to taste in a large saucepan. Cover and bring to a boil, then uncover, add the carrots and cook 2 minutes. Add the shrimp and cook until opaque, about 4 minutes. With a slotted spoon, transfer the carrots and shrimp to a colander and rinse under cold water. Return the water to a boil, add the scallops and cook until opaque, 1 to 2 minutes.

Remove the scallops with a slotted spoon, add to the colander and rinse under cold water. Ladle out 1/3 cup of the poaching liquid; set aside to cool. Dice half of the avocado and combine with the sliced celery, lettuce, capers and croûtons in a large bowl. Add the carrots, shrimp and scallops.

Puree the remaining avocado half in a blender with the reserved poaching liquid, the remaining lemon juice, chopped garlic, mayonnaise, 1/2 teaspoon salt, and pepper to taste. Toss with the salad and season with salt and pepper.

Oh, the irony...

Republicans don't see the irony and don't appreciate the "sour grapes."

Democrats see the irony throughout the actions of the Trump Administration.

Low-Bar Blonde Brownies

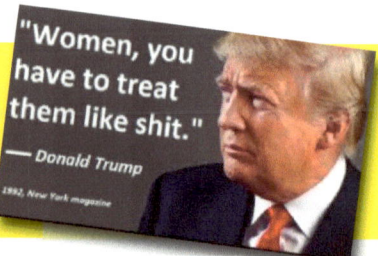

FUN FACT

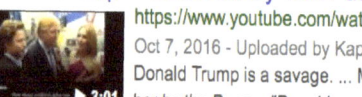

56

Low-Bar Blonde Brownies

Ingredients

1 cup all purpose Flour
1/2 tsp Baking Powder
1/4 tsp Baking Soda
1/2 tsp Salt

1 cup packed Brown Sugar
1/3 cup Butter (melted)
1 Egg
1 tbsp Vanilla
3 cup Semisweet Chocolate Chips

These are the lowest bars you will ever have...I hope.

Directions

Preheat oven to 350. Grease and flour a 9x9 pan (or triple the recipe and use a roasting pan... 11x17?). Mix together butter and sugar. Add egg and vanilla. Mix dry ingredients, then add to butter mixture. Fold in the chocolate chips. Spread evenly in the prepared pan. Bake for 20-25 minutes, until center is set. Alternatively, you may bake these as cookies by dropping 1/4 cupfuls onto a pan and baking for 15-17 minutes at 325.

 Bernie Sanders @SenSanders · 2m
"Trump's falsehoods are eroding public trust, at home and abroad." – @WSJ

FUN FACT

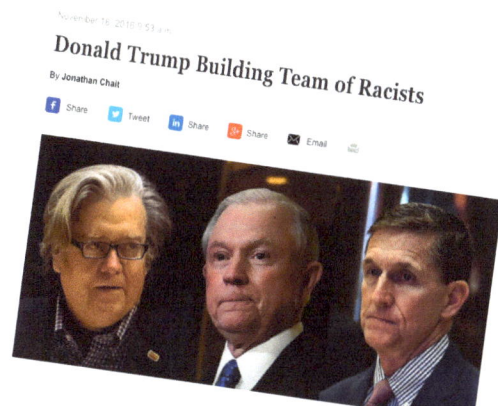

Republicans stand behind their champion and think we all need to give the new administration a chance to get it together.

Democrats are appalled at the POTUS behavior, general incompetencies, lack of qualified cabinet picks and the attempted cover-up ties with Russia. Some believe this bad behavior is setting a new-low precedence politically, while also eroding social norms.

Healthy Hummus Platter

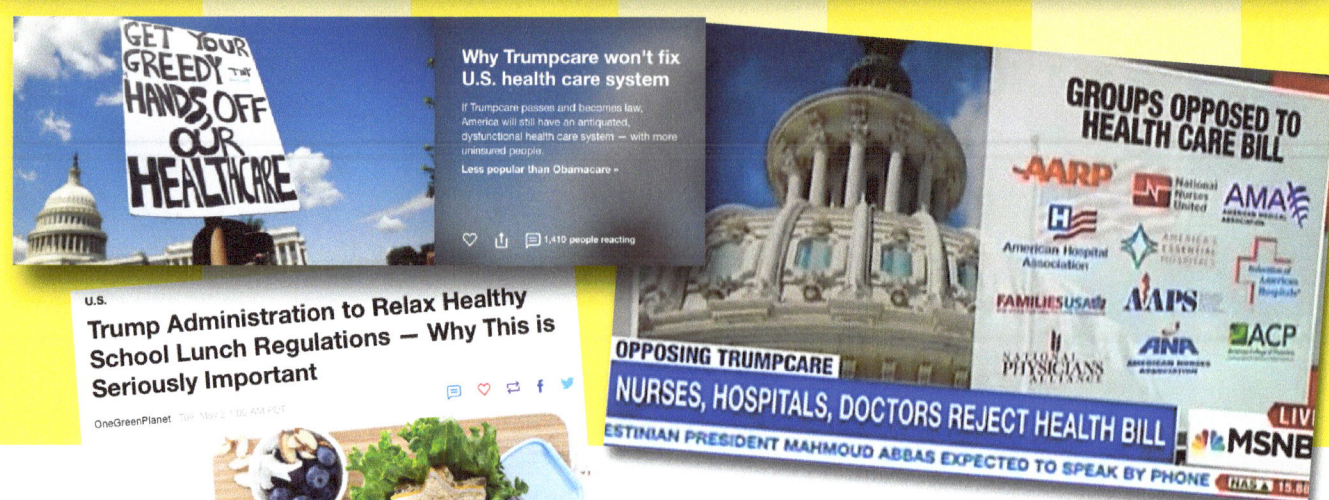

President Donald Trump has a number of unorthodox theories about politics, but his theory of why exercise is bad for you is the strangest I've heard yet.

"Other than golf, he considers exercise misguided, arguing that a person, like a battery, is born with a finite amount of energy,"

Healthy Hummus Platter

Ingredients

- 2 cups Chickpeas, drained
- 1/4 cup Olive Oil
- 2 cloves Garlic, minced
- 2 Tablespoons Hemp Seeds
- 1 tablespoon ground Cumin
- 1 tablespoon Hemp Seed Oil
- 1 teaspoon Paprika
- 1 teaspoon Lemon Juice
- Chopped fresh Parsley leaves

Eating well goes a long way - do what you can to keep yourself healthy as can be

Directions

Put everything except the parsley in a food processor and begin to process; add the chickpea liquid or water as needed to allow the machine to produce a smooth puree.

Drizzled with the olive oil and sprinkled with a bit more cumin or paprika and some parsley.

Short Version: Grab a bag of Cheetos, instead of that healthy stuff. And don't worry about those horrible healthy school lunches anymore. Michelle is out - Trump is in!

GOP still trying to CUT 880 Billion from Medicaid

Michelle Obama · 2/28/13
"We can give all our children the bright, healthy futures they so richly deserve." OFA.BO/RdDprw #LetsMove

 **Barack Obama** @BarackObama · 3h
Health care has always been about something bigger than politics: it's about the character of our country. facebook.com/barackobama/po…

Michelle Obama: The Business Case for Healthier...

 Elizabeth Warren @SenWarren · 3h
Throwing 24 million people off their health care to give billionaires a tax break is heartless & irresponsible. We cannot pass #Trumpcare.

Republicans aren't saying much, though the conservative sector wants to cut even more, while some moderate Republican officials are beginning to push back, to appease public outcry.

Democrats see the new healthcare bill as serving the wealthy and crippling the middle and lower class, the elderly, unemployed and people with pre-existing conditions...in short, the people who really need healthcare.

420 Green Guacamole Goodness

Hemp Blue Jeans Now Available on Amazon!

Colorado Celebrates Legalization Anniversary: Massive Drop in Arrests and Millions in Tax Revenue

By Art Way / AlterNet January 5, 2016

More than three years have passed since Colorado residents voted to legalize marijuana, which immediately allowed adults to possess and cultivate limited amounts of marijuana. This past New Year's Day marked the two year anniversary of adults being able to legally buy marijuana in Colorado. The policy is still in its formative stage, but the first year after marijuana sales started in Colorado went very well and we continue to see the good shape of things to come.

Donald Trump's presidential administration seems determined to bring the dark ages back to America's pot laws, leaving other countries to lead the world in cannabis legalization if America drops the ball.

Industrial Hemp
Paper Products
Construction Materials
Clothing
Medicinal

420 Green Guacamole Goodness

Ingredients

- 2 ripe Avocados
- 1/2 teaspoon salt
- 1 Tbsp lime juice/lemon juice
- 1 tablespoon Hemp Seed oil
- 4 Tbsp Diced Red Onion
- 3 tablespoons Cilantro
- 1 tablespoon chopped Jalapeno
- A dash of Black Pepper
- 1/2 Tomato, diced
- Serve with tortilla chips

Better double the ingredient amounts, because you're gonna want to snarf this up!

Directions

Scoop out the Avocado with a spoon.
Mash with a fork. Add the juice, hemp seed oil, chopped onion, cilantro, black pepper, and Jalapenos. Jalapeno peppers vary individually in their hotness. So, start with a half of one tablespoon of jalapeno pepper and add to the guacamole to your desired degree of hotness. Remember that much of this is done to taste because of the variability in the fresh ingredients. Wait...what was all of that at the end there... Better read it again....

Small Business And Independent Crafters Start-Ups

FreeSpiritHemp.com
for Healthy Hair & Skin

U.S. Smell The Truth
Germany, Israel ready to lead global marijuana legalization if Trump destroys p...
Respect states' legal-pot laws, Cantwell and Murray tell Attorney General Sessions The Seattle Times

Republican leaders think marijuana has no health benefits and consider it to be as harmful as heroin and cocaine (schedule 1) and are currently seeking to re-establish the harshest punishments.

Democrats see the value in hemp and marijuana for the local economy and for medicinal purposes. They also see the value in the generated taxes for infra-structure projects and educational funding.

GBLTQ

According to recent gay bullying statistics, gay and lesbian teens are two to three times as more likely to commit teen suicide than other youths. About 30 percent of all completed suicides have been related to sexual identity crisis. Students who also fall into the gay, bisexual, lesbian or transgendered identity groups report being five times as more likely to miss school because they feel unsafe after being bullied due to their sexual orientation. About 28 percent out of those groups feel forced to drop out of school altogether. Although more and more schools are working to crack down on problems with bullying, teens are still continuing to bully each other due to sexual orientation and other factors.

GBLTQ

Ingredients

1 Pkg Vegan Bacon
Bread slices of your choice...
but Rye, Pumpernickel, or a
Queersant is especially good...
just sayin'

Purple Cabbage
Spinach
Red Onion
Avocado (mashed or sliced)
or mayonnaise or whatever
YOU like!

A healthy and colorful blend of tastes in this one!

Directions

Use half of the package of vegan bacon for each sandwich (about 6 slices)
Heat up on a griddle/frying pan with a little olive oil to coat the surface.
Sprinkle lightly with seasoning salt IF desired, flip once and set griddle to LOW heat while you get the veggies together.

Lightly toast the bread.
Lay out bacon strips on the bread, then the spinach then the purple cabbage, then the red onion and then add the mayo/avocado - or do it in whatever order you like - **it's all good!**

> **GBLTQ - What does GBLTQ stand for? The Free Dictionary**
> acronyms.thefreedictionary.com/GBLTQ
> Acronym, Definition. **GBLTQ**, Gay, Bisexual, Lesbian, Transgendered, Questioning. **GBLTQ**, Gay, Bisexual, Lesbian, Transgendered, and Queer ...

Republicans are glad the right of gay people to marry is being blocked because their God/bible is not OK with it apparently. Their moto is "Don't Tread On Me" but it is OK to tread on other people's beliefs and freedoms if their particular bible edition or God says so.

Democrats believe in equal rights and no discrimination for all...Simple as that.

Budget-Cut Baked Beans

The rich would get a giant tax cut this year under GOP health-care plan
CNBC

GOP Obamacare repeal bill betrays key Trump campaign promise
Ethan Wolff-Mann

Gizmodo @Gizmodo · 1h
Trump's plan to slash the NIH budget won't just hurt scientists—it will hurt everyone. gizmo.do/OREOGsD

Trump budget envisions big cuts for health and human services
Los Angeles Times

Politics Money
Trump's Budget Eliminates These 19 Federal Agencies. Here's What They Do - and Cost
Meals on Wheels, financial aid, public media funding on chopping block in Trump budget CBS News

David Ward
@davidallenward
Anyone know where we got the money for 50 tomahawk missiles? I'm led to believe we are broke and can't afford education or healthcare.

Cuts to Human Services, Public Schools, Science and the Arts & more

Washington (CNN) President Donald Trump unveiled his first budget blueprint on Thursday, and to offset increases in defense spending, the President is proposing $54 billion in cuts to large parts of the federal government and popular programs big and small.

Trump's budget would cut off funding entirely for several agencies, including arts, public broadcasting and development groups, and also proposes steep cuts to agencies like the State Department and Environmental Protection Agency.

Virtually every agency will see some sort of cut, with only Defense, Homeland Security and Veterans Affairs getting a boost. Congress will have the final say, and lawmakers have already expressed opposition to many of the proposals.

Trump budget envisions big cuts for health and human services - LA ...
www.latimes.com/.../la-na-essential-washington-updates-trump-budget-envisions-big-...
13 hours ago - **Trump** would also **cut** $4.2 billion in grants the federal **government** provides to communities to assist poor people, including the decades-old ...

Could Trump's 2018 budget kill Sesame Street's beloved Big Bird?
USA Today · 14 hours ago

Good-Bye Big Bird, we'll miss you!

Joy Reid ✓
@JoyAnnReid

Seriously, what kind of person wakes up in the morning thinking, let's cut Meals on Wheels! And Sesame Street!!? Unreal.
#TrumpBudget
7:46 AM - 16 Mar 2017

 Follow

Politics Washington Post
In his first budget, Trump to struggling seniors: You'll be on you own
Get There | Perspective When people talk about retirement, they often muse about traveling the world, playing golf or visiting with grandchildren. But the truth is many seniors won't spend "golden" retirement years like they are on a long vacation. Instead they will be working because they can't afford to retire. Or they'll fret about...

Budget-Cut Baked Beans

Ingredients

1 can of Baked Beans

Optional
(if you can afford it)
2 Tablespoons Brown Sugar
(if you are doing really well)
2 Hot Dogs cooked, sliced

Feel "Great Again" with a nice big helping of Budget Baked Beans!

Directions

Heat the beans and optional ingredients in a pan over medium heat, a fire-pit, or in a bowl and bring to the microwave at the nearest 7-11 convenience store.

$880 BILLION to be CUT from Medicaid

President's cuts to Interior: $1.5 billion
President's check to Park Service: $77K
Park Ranger's face: Priceless

FUN FACT

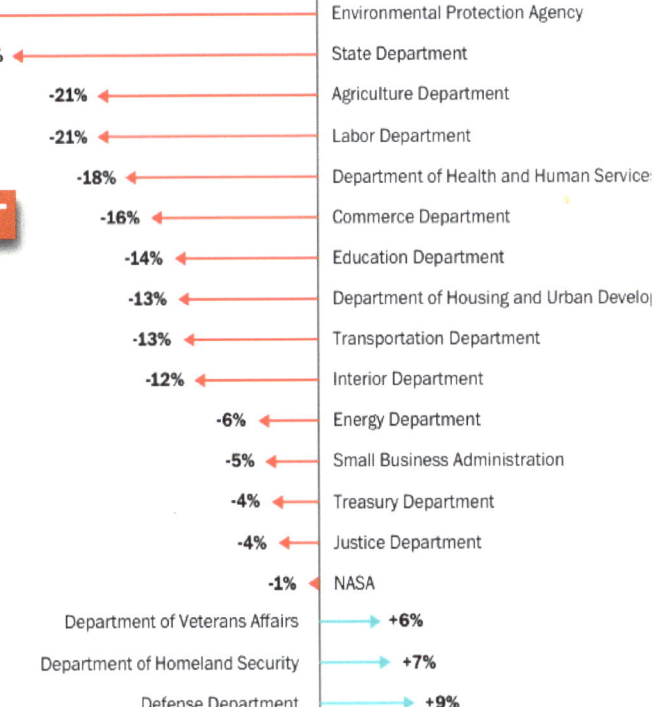

- -31% Environmental Protection Agency
- -29% State Department
- -21% Agriculture Department
- -21% Labor Department
- -18% Department of Health and Human Services
- -16% Commerce Department
- -14% Education Department
- -13% Department of Housing and Urban Development
- -13% Transportation Department
- -12% Interior Department
- -6% Energy Department
- -5% Small Business Administration
- -4% Treasury Department
- -4% Justice Department
- -1% NASA
- Department of Veterans Affairs +6%
- Department of Homeland Security +7%
- Defense Department +9%

Republicans applaud budget cuts and are happy to see less "hand-outs" (even though many of them are on welfare themselves).

Democrats are not happy with the cuts and want public service programs including help for the homeless, elderly, disabled, as well as funding for environmental protection, research and training agencies, to be properly funded.

Reverse Rice Pudding

He has changed his position on a dozen key promises and positions, our analysis found

He's reversed tough talk on labeling China a "currency manipulator" and the North Atlantic Treaty Organization as "obsolete." He's spent numerous weekends away from the White House at his private Florida retreat, after years of lambasting President Barack Obama for traveling on taxpayer dollars. And he is outpacing Obama's time on the green. And despite his campaign rallying cry to "drain the swamp," Trump has filled his White House staff and Cabinet with billionaires, donors, former politicians and Wall Street financiers.

See our list of Trump reversals in his first 100 days:
1. On whether NATO is obsolete
Before becoming president: "NATO is obsolete." (April 4, 2016)
Since becoming president: NATO is "no longer obsolete." (April 12, 2017)
2. On White House transparency
Before becoming president: "Why is @BarackObama spending millions to try and hide his records? He is the least transparent President--ever--and he ran on transparency." (June 6, 2012)
Since becoming president: The White House won't release its visitor logs, reversing an Obama-era policy. (April 2017)
3. On whether he will have time to play golf
Before becoming president: "I'm going to be working for you. I'm not going to have time to go play golf." (August 8, 2016)
Since becoming president: Has played golf at least 14 times since taking office. (as of April 17, 2017)
4. On presidential travel
Before becoming president: "We pay for Obama's travel so he can fundraise millions so Democrats can run on lies. Then we pay for his golf."
Since becoming president: Spent more than half of first 13 weekends as president at his resort in Mar-a-Lago, likely costing millions of taxpayer dollars. (as of April 18, 2017)
5. On attacking Syria after a chemical weapons attack
Before becoming president: "AGAIN, TO OUR VERY FOOLISH LEADER, DO NOT ATTACK SYRIA - IF YOU DO MANY VERY BAD THINGS WILL HAPPEN & FROM THAT FIGHT THE U.S. GETS NOTHING!"

(this list goes on, look it up)

Reverse Rice Pudding

Ingredients

Rice Pudding
Raspberries
Blackberries

Blueberries

Do a U-Turn for this not-so-good, well it's-pretty-good, then again... Reverse Rice Pudding

Directions

Make rice pudding according to package directions. Top with fresh raspberries, blackberries and blueberries - well... then again, forget the pudding. Use a gallon of vanilla ice cream instead - no cooking necessary...but if you wanted to cook, you could do so if you really wanted to... but it's a waste of time really...but freshly made pudding...there is nothing better, I'll tell you that... but cake is good too. I know the best chocolate you've ever seen.

Politics Salon.com
Donald Trump doesn't like the "archaic" Constitution: "It's really a bad thing for the country"
President Donald Trump has already made it clear that he's upset about how the job of being president isn't as easy as he thought it would be. Now the president and his chief of staff ar...

...Yet More Threats of a Government Shutdown ...or not...

Up First ✓ @UpFirst · 2h
After Republicans compromised with Democrats to avoid a shutdown, President Trump tweeted that the "country needs a good shutdown."

Republicans have faith in "The Donald," even if he does the opposite of some of the things he promised he'd do. He can do no wrong in their eyes. "USA! USA! USA!"

Democrats slip further and further into the surreal and bizarre Trump Land of their nightmares.

Media Mash-Up

"That was some weird shit!"
~ Bush 43 on Trump's inaugural address

The eye-roll heard 'round the world

Media Mash-Up

Ingredients

- Red Potatoes
- Golden Potatoes
- Purple Potatoes
- 1/4 cup milk
- 3 tablespoons Coconut Oil
- Minced Garlic
- Chives
- Sage
- Oregano
- Salt
- Crushed Red Pepper

"Comfort Food"... for trying times

Directions

Wash and boil the potatoes until tender. Drain. Smash and mash the potatoes including the skin. Add half and half cream/milk and Coconut Oil. Medium heat. Stir. Add remain ingredients and continue to mash it all up together. We are all curious to see how it comes out.

You gotta love this fulfilling and tasty dish. Filled with a tantalizing variety of potatoes and an array of intriguing spices. It is the ultimate comfort food with a kick. Enjoy!

World · ThinkProgress
Spicer says Trump didn't say what Trump literally said
More gaslighting from the White House. In his press conference on Monday, White House Press Secretary Sean Spicer directly contradicted President Donald Trump's comments...

 **Trump's 'look' at changing libel law is going absolutely nowhere**
CNN

 **White House seeks quick vote on healthcare overhaul but hurdles remain**
Reuters

Republicans feel Trump is being treated unfairly by the late night talk-show hosts and the news media (except FOX News).

Democrats are just watching what seems to be a train wreck that they can't look away from. At least they gain a little comic relief while making yet another batch of Swampwater Martinis.

Cluster Fudge

Paul Ryan calls confusion on Trump's travel ban rollout 'regrettable,' but says he supports it
Jacob Pramuk | @jacobpramuk
Tuesday, 31 Jan 2017 | 10:31 AM ET
CNBC

Politics Business Insider
War breaks out between the Steve Bannon and Jared Kushner factions in the White...

NPR @NPR · 2h
Trump reverses his 2016 campaign stance on NATO: "I said it was obsolete; it's no longer obsolete"

Congress just killed your Internet privacy protections **FUN FACT**
money.cnn.com/2017/03/28/technology/house-internet... ▼
Mar 27, 2017 · The future of **online privacy** is now in President Trump's hands. The House of Representatives voted Tuesday to repeal **Internet privacy** protections that were ...

Trump, In A 180-Degree Switch, Says NATO 'No Longer Obsolete'
President Trump, who has questioned the relevance of NATO and challenged allies to spend more on their own defense, met on Wednesd...
npr.org

Scientific American @ @... · 1h
A discussion of climate change was notably absent from Trump's meeting with Chinese President Xi. (By @dbiello)

China's Xi Outshines Trump as the World's Future Energ...
scientificamerican.com

Bernie Sanders @SenSanders · 3h
We should be moving toward decriminalization of marijuana, not reverting progress that states have made.

White House: Feds will step up marijuana law enforcement
The White House said Thursday it expects law enforcement agents to enforce federal marijuana laws when they come into conflict with states ...
cnn.com

Politics International Business Times
Alt-right turns on Donald Trump over Syria missile attack

Live updates: Reaction to U.S. missile strike in Syria over chemical attack Yahoo News

70

Cluster Fudge

Ingredients

3 cups semisweet chocolate chips
1 can sweetened condensed milk
1/4 cup butter
1 cup chopped walnuts

Nothing says cluster, like ...fudge

Directions

Place chocolate chips, sweetened condensed milk, and butter or margarine in large microwaveable bowl. Zap in microwave on medium until chips are melted, about 3-5 minutes, stirring once or twice during cooking. Stir in nuts Pour into well-greased 8x8-inch glass baking dish. Refrigerate until set.

Republicans think everything is just fine in Trump Land and they are happy that America is becoming great again and they are no longer oppressed.

Democrats think there are a lot of serious issues and incompetence within the Trump Administration.

Cover-Up Casserole

"If you're not guilty of a crime, what do you need immunity for?"

Jeff Sessions Must Resign as Attorney General Whether or not he perjured himself on the Russia matter, Sessions must go

The Washington Post reported Wednesday that Attorney General Jeff Sessions made inaccurate statements under oath about his contacts with Russian officials in his confirmation hearing. Asked what he would do if he learned of contacts between the Trump campaign and the Russian government.

 Donald J. Trump ✓ @realDonaldTrump · 9h
James Comey better hope that there are no "tapes" of our conversations before he starts leaking to the press!

72

Cover-Up Casserole

Ingredients

2 lbs Hamburger
4 cups Mashed Potatoes
2 cups Mixed Vegetables
1 Cup Shredded Cheddar Cheese

The best tasting Cover-Up Casserole, this side of the Atlantic!

Directions

Cook the hamburger with medium heat and a little oil (stove top)
Add the vegetables, mix together and then place in a baking pan or baking dish.
Smooth out evenly and then sprinkle the shredded cheese over the hamburg/veggie mix
Carefully spoon the mashed potatoes over the hamburg/veggie/cheese mix
Be sure to cover it up completely - the hamburger, that is...

 **Donald J. Trump** @realDonaldTrump · 10h
Again, the story that there was collusion between the Russians & Trump campaign was fabricated by Dems as an excuse for losing the election.

Republican response is that there is nothing to cover-up and even if there were, it would be to "Make America Great Again." (still don't know what period of time they are referring to)

Democrats are very concerned about the extent and topics of Russian communications. They want a full and impartial investigation about the communications and the Trump Administration's attempted interference with FBI reports.

Safe-Again Stir-Fry

Gizmodo ✓ @Gizmodo · 2h
With attack on Syria, Trump alienates the alt-right gizmo...

NPR ✓ @NPR · 4h
Multiple polls show rising support for the Affordable Care Act as GOP moves toward keeping the promise of repeal

Americans Conflicted Over GOP Plans To Dump Obamacare
Growing public support for the Affordable Care Act seems to be at odds with the GOP's plans to repeal and replace it.

The Guardian ✓ @guardian · 18m
North Korea warns 'thermonuclear war may break out at any moment'

North Korea warns 'thermonuclear war may break out at any moment'
Country's deputy UN ambassador Kim In-ryong
Trump tells Kim Jong-un he has 'call...
theguardian

Trump considering military response against Assad
The president huddled with his top advisers to discuss how to punish the Syrian leader after a chemic...
'Looking at a range of options' »

U.S. deploys naval strike group to Korean Peninsula
The strike group includes the Nimitz-class aircraft supercarrier USS Carl Vinson, two-guided...
Increased presence necessary »

♡ ↑↓ 💬 4302 people reacting

"Make America Safe Again!"
...so how's that workin' out for ya...

World Reuters
Russia warns of serious consequences from U.S. strike in Syria
Trump is doing what Obama failed to – punishing Assad for using chemical weapons in Syria International Business Times

World The Huffington Post
After Mosul Falls, Trump Loses Influence In Iraq
TRMS Exclusive: DHS document undermines Trump case for travel ban MSNBC

 Hillary Clinton and 3 others follow

Bernie Sanders ✓ @BernieSanders · Apr 9
It is easy to go to war with other countries. It is not so easy to comprehend the unintended consequences of that war.

World Newsweek
North Korea Threatens 'Merciless Attack' As U.S. and South Korea Conduct Drills
North Korea threatens to use 'nuclear sword of justice' against US–South Korea military drills International Business Times UK

If President Trump sends our children into another reckless war... these **BETTER BE** the first volunteers to enlist.
Occupy Democrats

World CNBC Videos
North Korea is warning the US of a nuclear strike
China, South Korea discuss more sanctions on North Korea amid talk of Trump action Reuters

How a single Trump sentence enraged S. Korea
Trump's apparently offhand comment while meeting with China's president, that "Korea actually used to be a part of China," has upset many.
The history »

World Reuters
U.S. says time to act on North Korea, China says not up to Beijing alone
By Michelle Nichols and Lesley Wroughton UNITED NATIONS (Reuters) - U.S. Secretary of State Rex Tillerson warned on Friday that failure to curb North Kore...

Trump says North Korea's Kim is 'a pretty smart cookie'

North Korea test-fires ballistic missile in defiance of world pressure

Safe-Again Stir-Fry

Ingredients

- 2 Cups Snowpeas
- 1 Sliced Red Bell Pepper
- 1 Sliced Yellow Bell Pepper
- 1 Sliced Green Bell Pepper
- 1 Small Red Onion
- 1 Cup Diced Cauliflower
- Diced Sage
- Diced Rosemary

Toss it all together and see how it turns out. But don't worry, everything is OK.

Directions

Heat some oil in a large, heavy skillet over medium-high heat. Add some chunks of onion and chunks of bell pepper. The veggies you use in this dish are up to you. Just add the firmer veggies first, to give them a chance to cook.

Short Version: Just order delivery - probably safer to stay inside at this point anyway.

World Yahoo News UK
"Chaotic" Trump administration could start war with North Korea, warns former MI6...
North Korea state media warns of nuclear strike if provoked as U.S. warships approach Reuters

World Defense One
Russia Has Deployed a Treaty-Violating Missile. Here's What the US Should Do
Russia has begun to deploy a nuclear-capable, ground-launched cruise missile, contrary to its obligations under the...

World The Street
Russian Warship Moves Toward U.S. Navy Ships That Launched Syria Strikes
US launches military strike on Syrian air base ABC News

World Associated Press
Russia, Iran and Syria issue warning to US
Germany and E.U. Allies Condemn Russia, But View its Support as Necessary For 'Political Solution' to Syria CNS News

Edward Snowden @Snowden · 8h
Bitter lesson:
When any government conceals knowledge of vulnerabilities in common software, those vulns will be found and used by enemies.

Republicans feel safe again now that they have bombed Syria and have heated conflicts with North Korea and Russia...and are happy that there are less gun restrictions and NOBODY IS GONNA TAKE THEIR GUNS AWAY!

Democrats did not want Bush's war and do not want more costly conflicts. They feel less safe on many levels - nationally and even within their own neighborhoods as hate/crime rate increase in some areas.

Odd Orange Greens

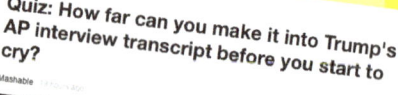

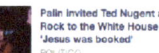

What's wrong with this picture?

Odd Orange Greens

Ingredients

Arugula
Carrots
Beets
Edemame
Cucumber

Oranges (slices or sections)
top with Sunflower seeds
Black Sesame Seeds
and Crispy Soba Noodles.
Raspberry Vinaigrette

What is this even supposed to be? Odd Orange Greens...just going along for the ride at this point.

Directions

Chop all vegetables, slice the orange and toss it all together for Odd Orange Greens.
I really don't even know what to say at this point.
Good Luck with that one.

Poll: Does Trump's support have a ceiling — or a floor? - CBS News
www.cbsnews.com/.../nation-tracker-poll-does-trump-support-have-a-ceiling-or-a-flo... ▼
Feb 12, 2017 - A single **poll** number can't always answer those puzzles, so here we ... They put no conditions on their support: "I'm a **Trump supporter**, period. ← **Bottom Line**

Politics CNBC.com
Trump: 'People don't ask that question, but why was there a Civil War?'
President Donald Trump questioned why the American Civil War couldn't have been avoided during an interview on SiriusXM, according to an excerpt published on The Hill. President...

Republicans are a little overwhelmed with the various incidents, but continue to stand by their champion, though a few may be beginning to question one or two incidents.

Democrats are hoping they are in a coma and are just having a really weird and bad dream, were they are paralyzed while watching a chain of seeming never-ending destructive events.

Unintelligible Upside-Down Cake

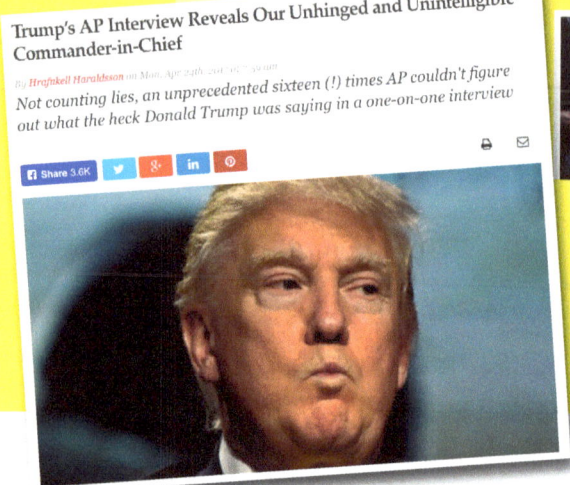

TRUMP: So the Republican Party has various groups, all great people. They're great people. But some are moderate, some are very conservative. The Democrats don't seem to have that nearly as much. You know the Democrats have, they don't have that. The Republicans do have that. And I think it's fine. But you know there's a pretty vast area in there. And I have a great relationship with all of them. Now, we have government not closing. I think we'll be in great shape on that. It's going very well. Obviously, that takes precedent.

AP: That takes precedent over health care? For next week?

TRUMP: Yeah, sure. Next week. Because the hundred days is just an artificial barrier. The press keeps talking about the hundred days. But we've done a lot. You have a list of things. I don't have to read it.

AP: You did put out though, as a candidate, you put out a 100-day plan. Do you feel like you should be held accountable to that plan?

TRUMP: Somebody, yeah, somebody put out the concept of a hundred-day plan. But yeah. Well, I'm mostly there on most items. Go over the items, and I'll talk to you …

(Crosstalk.)
TRUMP: But things change. There has to be flexibility. Let me give you an example. President Xi, we have a, like, a really great relationship. For me to call him a currency manipulator and then say, "By the way, I'd like you to solve the North Korean problem," doesn't work. So you have to have a certain flexibility, Number One. Number Two, from the time I took office till now, you know, it's a very exact thing. It's not like generalities. Do you want a Coke or anything?

AP: I'm OK, thank you. No. …

TRUMP: But President Xi, from the time I took office, he has not, they have not been currency manipulators. Because there's a certain respect because he knew I would do something or whatever. But more importantly than him not being a currency manipulator the bigger picture, bigger than even currency manipulation, if he's helping us with North Korea, with nuclear and all of the things that go along with it, who would call, what am I going to do, say, "By the way, would you help us with North Korea? And also, you're a currency manipulator." It doesn't work that way.

AP: Right.

78

Unintelligible Upside-Down Cake

Ingredients

1/4 cup Butter
1 cup packed Brown Sugar
1 can Pineapple slices
1 jar maraschino Cherries

1 box Yellow Cake Mix

Vegetable oil and eggs called for on cake mix box

Don't try to understand it - It's great - Believe me!

Directions

Heat oven to 350°F (325°F for dark or nonstick pan). In 13x9-inch pan, melt butter in oven. Sprinkle brown sugar evenly over butter. Arrange pineapple slices on brown sugar. Place cherry in center of each pineapple slice, and arrange remaining cherries around slices; press gently into brown sugar. Add enough water to reserved pineapple juice to measure 1 cup. Make cake batter as directed on box, substituting pineapple juice mixture for the water. Pour batter over pineapple and cherries. Bake 42 to 48 minutes (44 to 53 minutes for dark or nonstick pan) or until toothpick inserted in center comes out clean. Immediately run knife around side of pan to loosen cake. Place heatproof serving plate upside down onto pan; turn plate and pan over. Leave pan over cake 5 minutes so brown sugar topping can drizzle over cake; remove pan. Cool 30 minutes.

Business CNN

A fatal flaw in Trump's tax cut: Senate rules

The JCT analysis concluded that a cut, to 20%, put in place for only three years would result in a "nonnegligible revenue loss in the tax years immediately following the budget window."...

 Trump's tax cut hopes face an uphill battle
AFP

 House Budget Committee chair: It's time for tax cuts, reform
FOX News Videos

World CNBC.com

China is sending the US a new message about North Korea

China is calling for restraint as a US strike group moves toward Korean waters   Monday, 24 Apr 2017 | 10:15 AM ET | 00:44 Beijing appears to be sending fresh signals about its view o...

 Xi Urges Restraint on North Korea in Phone Call With Trump
Bloomberg

 Could North Korea Really Back Up Its Threat and Sink a U.S. Carrier?
Esquire

Republicans feel they know exactly what he means and not necessarily what he says (just like when they talk to God). Most think Trump is being judged too harshly.

Democrats believe Trump is incompetent and should be removed from office - a danger to national security, the economy and society.

Ridiculous Red Radish Tuna

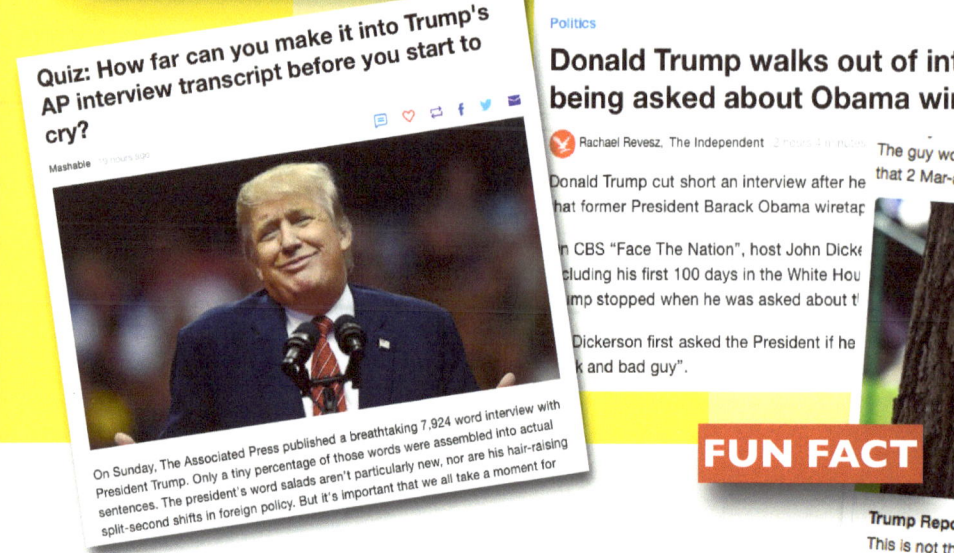

FUN FACT

Donald Trump cut short an interview Rachael Revesz, The Independent 2 hours 4 minutes ago

after he was pushed to explain his allegations that former President Barack Obama wiretapped his phone. On CBS "Face The Nation", host John Dickerson pressed Mr Trump on various topics including his first 100 days in the White House and his new health care plans, but Mr Trump stopped when he was asked about the alleged wiretap.

Mr Dickerson first asked the President if he stood by his claim that Mr Obama was a "sick and bad guy". Barack Obama calls out Donald Trump's 'ridiculous' wiretapping claims **"I don't stand by anything,"** he replied. "I just – you can take it the way you want. I think our side's been proven very strongly. And everybody's talking about it. And frankly it should be discussed. I think that is a very big surveillance of our citizens. I think it's a very big topic. And it's a topic that should find out what the hell is going on." The host then pushed Mr Trump to explain further, but the President cut him off, responding, "You don't have to ask me."

"Why not?" Mr Dickerson asked.

"Because I have my own opinions. You can have your own opinions."

"But you're the President of the United States," the host countered.

Mr Trump then decided to stop the interview, saying, "Ok, it's enough. Thank you."

 Donald J. Trump  Follow
@realDonaldTrump

How low has President Obama gone to tapp my phones during the very sacred election process. This is Nixon/Watergate. Bad (or sick) guy!

5:02 AM - 4 Mar 2017

Politics Business Insider

Sean Spicer angrily defends Trump's wiretap claims in wild, contentious press...

White House repeats claim British spy agency monitored Trump   AFP

Ridiculous Red Radish Tuna

Ingredients

- 1 Can of Solid Albacore Tuna
- 1 Bunch of Fresh Spinach
- 2 Radishes, sliced
- 2 Tbsp Red Onion, diced
- 2 tbsp Mayonnaise
- Oregano
- Ground Sage
- Course Ground Sea Salt
- Course Ground Black Pepper
- Hemp Seed Oil or Olive Oil

Ridiculously good Red Radish Tuna

Directions

Dice the onion, slice the radishes and mix up the tuna.
Arrange the spinach leaves flat on plate or in a bowl.
Put a scoop or two of tuna in the middle, then arrange the radish slices around the tuna.
Sprinkle with seasonings and drizzle with olive oil or hemp seed oil.

Republicans are noticing some of Trump's ...incidents but most think it's a "Witch Hunt" like they say on FOX news and like what Trump says in his tweets.

Democrats still don't seem to be able to do much about it anyway...

Comedic Cornbread Catfish

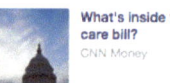

FUN FACT

Comedic Cornbread Catfish

Ingredients

4 catfish fillets, skin removed
Creole Seasoning Salt

2 cups all-purpose flour
1 cup cornmeal
Oil, for frying

Comedic Catfish goes great with a Swampwater Martini or Protester Punch!

Directions

Heat a fryer or a deep pot halfway filled with oil to 350 degrees. Dredge the catfish in the flour mixture and place in fryer. Deep fry for approximately 7 to 8 minutes until done. Drain on paper towels.

Some 'Catty' responses to #AskTrump...

 Amanda

When you get hold of the person whose idea this was, will there be hell toupee?

#AskTrump

 cait

#AskTrump when you "deport all immigrants" where will your wife be going?

 **Rob Cordero**

#AskTrump can you confirm or deny the rumor that you're really just two children stacked on top of each other in a trench coat?

Republicans have to 'grin and bear it' if they want to watch literally any late night talk show that routinely lambastes the POTUS and his administration.

Democrats find a sense of camaraderie when they tune into late night talk shows and admittedly appreciate the comic relief.

83

Delusional Dill Chicken

The Trump Crew @Trump_Crew · 8h
Before Donald Trump was elected the USA was on it's way to become a totalitarian state of socialism, collectivism and division!
#MAGA

Politics The Independent
Donald Trump's mental health 'keeps getting worse', Washington insiders claim
Concerns over Donald Trump's mental status are taking hold in Washington and the media after the latest report that he leaked classified information to Russian officials...

 Russia intelligence leaks aim at Donald Trump, but wound America — USA Today

 Why Trump's Russia-ISIS slip is unprecedented in U.S. presidential history — Newsweek

Trump sets out on 2020 Campaign Trail
(one month after inauguration)

Politics CNBC
President Trump says if election were held now 'I would win by a lot more than I did on November 8'
"I think we're doing a great job," President Trump tells NBC News.

'We finally agree': Trump digs up old Rosie O'Donnell tweet to back Comey firing — Yahoo News

Conyers: Sessions' part in Comey firing may violate ethics rules — Detroit Free Press

willful ignorance

(noun)
The practice or act of intentional and blatant avoidance, disregard or disagreement with facts, empirical evidence and well-founded arguements because they oppose or contradict your own existing personal beliefs.

This practice is most commonly found in the political or religious ideologies of "<u>conservative</u>" <u>Americans</u>.

 **Deplorable Skip** 🇺🇸
@Deplorable_Skip   [Follow]

Trump is now recognized overseas as a powerful leader & America as a respected country. At home FAKE NEWS claims his rating is down to 37%. 😂

Mary Baker @SolidWords · 33m
Replying to @Deplorable_Skip
Meanwhile, ABROAD Israel is furious, Germany laughing, and Russia smug. China is building giant Trump chickens, and AUS wants no part of us.

Son of Liberty @davidcmcalpine · Jun 7
Replying to @billoreilly @muchmoresalt
Civil war is brewing. Time for **Trump** supporters to **exercise** their 2nd Amendment Rights. Get lots of ammo & survival food too! It's coming.

 **Josh Stein** @Jstein1202 · Jun 14
Replying to @funder @SpeakerRyan
Guns don't kill people, shooters don't kill people, Democrats **exercise** of free speech critical of **trump** kill people. Got it 🙄

84

Delusional Dill Chicken

Ingredients

2 skinless Chicken Breasts
1 tablespoon Flour
1 pinch Salt
1 pinch Pepper
1 teaspoon Butter
1 teaspoon Vegetable Oil
1/4 cup White Wine

1 tablespoon Fresh Dill
2 teaspoons Green Onions
1/2 teaspoon Lemon Juice
Dill Sprigs (to garnish)

Delusional Dill Chicken... because delusion tastes so good!

Directions

Dredge the chicken breasts lightly in flour; season with a pinch each of salt and pepper.
In a skillet, heat butter and oil over medium-high heat; cook chicken, turning once, for about 6 minutes or until golden brown and no longer pink inside.
Remove from the pan and keep warm. Pour off all the fat from the pan. Pour in the wine and bring to a boil over high heat; cook, stirring for about 1 minute or until reduced and syrupy.
Add the cream; boil for about 1 minute or until thick enough to coat a spoon.
Stir in the dill, chives, lemon juice, and salt and pepper to taste.
Stir any accumulated juices from the chicken back into the pan; pour the sauce over the chicken.
Garnish with lemon slices and dill sprigs.

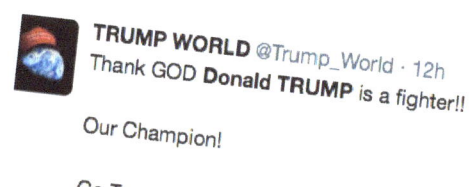

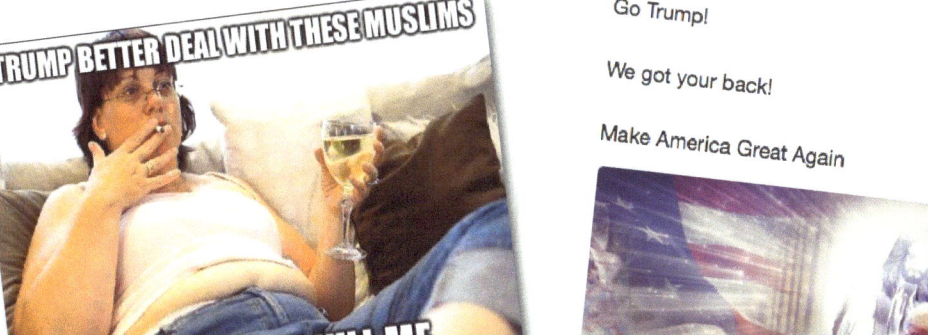

Republicans think everything is becoming great again though they still won't specify as to what time period they are referring to.

Democrats are wondering just what would it take....I mean really....WTF?

Cyber Smoothie

Cyberspace
is still very new (from a legal and policy point of view)

In the modern form, the internet and cyberspace have existed for only about 25 years and have constantly changed over that time period. Therefore, we have not developed the comprehensive frameworks we need. In fact, we don't yet have clear answers to key questions:

What is the right division of responsibility between governments and the private sector in terms of defense?
What standard of care should we expect companies to exercise in handling our data?
How should regulators approach cyber security in their industries?
What actions are acceptable for governments, companies, and individuals to take and which actions are not?

How do we hold individuals and organizations accountable across international boundaries?

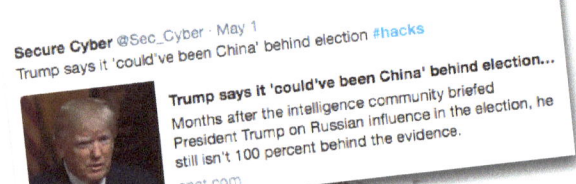

 Edward Snowden @Snowden · 3h
In light of today's attack, Congress needs to be asking @NSAgov if it knows of any other vulnerabilities in software used in our hospitals.

· 2h
 Not sure when govs will start taking **cyber** security seriously. Maybe after someone **hacks** electricity grids.

World New York Post
Anonymous warns world to 'prepare' for World War 3
The infamous hacktivist group Anonymous has released a chilling new video - urging people across the globe to "prepare" for World War 3 - as the US and North Korea...

Cyber Smoothie

Ingredients

1/2 Milk (Almond or Soy)
1 Banana
1/2 cup Raspberries
1/2 Blackberries
1/2 Blueberries

1/2 Strawberries
3 cups of Ice
1/2 cup Vodka or Rum
(not optional)

Make a big batch of Cyber Smoothies and contemplate a virtual reality.

Directions

Wash all fruit and place in a blender.
Add liquid ingredients and walnuts, blend on high, then add the ice and blend again. Shut off the wifi, shutdown your apps and unplug your laptops - enjoy this Cyber Smoothie incognito.

Short Version: Pick up a few smoothies at the store and add some ice and Vodka...or Rum...or both....it's been a long day....

GOP rolls back Obama's on-line privacy regulations. Your personal information won't be as personal as you may like. **FUN FACT**

Republicans are more concerned about cyber-leaks within their own administration right now. Trump has a vendetta against "leakers" now.

Democrats choose rum as an optional ingredient and are more than willing to test the cyber-security of this berry laden beverage until they are sure everything is OK.

Turmoil Turkey Pinwheels

Turmoil Turkey Pinwheels

Ingredients

- 1 Tortilla (spinach, tomato, plain)
- 3 Turkey (sliced)
- 2 tablespoons Cream Cheese (onion chive or other)
- 1/2 cup fresh Spinach, Dandelion, Kale
- ground Sage
- Italian Seasoning
- Olive Oil

Take a break away from all the turmoil and enjoy these Turmoil Turkey Pinwheels! (You're gonna need your strength)

Directions

Spread the cream cheese over the tortilla and then lay down the turkey slices.
Top with spinach, etc. Sprinkle seasonings and drizzle olive oil.
Roll tortilla and cut into 1-inch slices.

Note: Goes nicely with Meanwhile Mojitos.

Spicer: Trump knows exactly what 'covfefe' tweet meant
The White House press secretary offers an unexpected answer when asked about the president's viral, now deleted tweet.
'Small group of people know' »

BBC News (World) @B... · 4h
We asked three American Civil War historians to parse @POTUS Trump's comments, line by line.
Civil War historians take on Trump - BBC News
bbc.co.uk

Politics Newsweek
Donald Trump's Latest Approval Rating Plunges to New Low (Even Before Comey Memo Surfaced)
Some bad news for the White House: The latest approval rating poll from Morning Consult/Politico released Wednesday found President Donald Trump has hit its lowe...

Moby To Trump: "Just Resign, Ok?"
Stereogum

Why Donald Trump Is Wrong About Exercise
LiveScience.com

BBC News (World) @B... · 5h
Trump says he misses life before he became US president
Trump says he misses life before he became US presi...
bbc.co.uk

Republicans still stand behind Trump and Fox News. Nothing but a lot of "Witch Hunts!"

Democrats are sickened, out-raged, disgusted and angry, but STILL can't seem to do much about it.

Crispy Chaos Calamari

Politics Vox.com
Trump is threatening to release secret Comey "tapes" and cancel press briefings
Friday morning, President Trump took to Twitter to launch a series of bizarre complaints - beginning with the allegation that the entire Russia issue was fabricate...

 Sean Spicer Returns to White House Press Briefings After Hiding in Bush, Navy Reserv... Newsweek

 Spicer dodges questions ove Trump's 'tapes' tweet during press briefing ABC News Videos

 Why Fox News anchor bashed Conway's credibility
"Well, history," says Shep Smith, dismissing Kellyanne Conway's defense of the president's wiretapping allegations.
'Fox News can now confirm microwaves heat food' »
♡ ⬆ 💬 1182 people reacting

Trump threatens Comey on Twitter
President Trump suggests that his private conversations with the former FBI director may have been recorded.
'Better hope...' »
♡ ⬆ 💬 12.7k people reacting

cha·os
/ˈkāˌäs/ 🔊

noun

complete disorder and confusion.
"snow caused chaos in the region"
synonyms: disorder, disarray, disorganization, confusion, mayhem, bedlam, pandemonium, havoc, turmoil, tumult, commotion, disruption, upheaval, uproar, maelstrom; More

- PHYSICS

    behavior so unpredictable as to appear random, owing to great sensitivity to small changes in conditions.

 **Molly**   Apr 13
If the people investigating Trump's collusion with Russia could hurry the fuck up before he starts World War III that would be GREAT.

Politics The Week
Trump reportedly blames Sean Spicer for his James Comey disaster
Apparently President Trump can't even scream at his TV set without somebody leaking it to reporters, so it's little surprise to learn that Trump is polling confidantes...

 **Trump tweets: Suggests Comey leaked to the press, calls Russia inquiry 'witch...** Los Angeles Times

Donald Trump Threatens James Comey, Implies He Taped Conversations The Huffington Post

Donald Trump has offended every foreign country he's about to visit
Donald Trump is off on his first foreign tour as US president and he's taking a whole lot of baggage with him. And that's just his family.

 **Will Donald Trump break his Jerusalem promise?** International Business Times

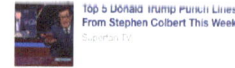 **Top 5 Donald Trump Punch Lines From Stephen Colbert This Week** SuperstarTV

Politics Business Insider
The White House's decision to let only a Russian photographer into Trump's Oval Office meeting has turne...
By barring all press but a Russian photographer from President Donald Trump's meeting with...

 How Russian State Media Got Exclusive Access to the Oval Office Newsweek

 White House insists Russian state photographers didn't bug the Oval Office during Putin-... The Week

Business The Week
Fox News scandal spreads, reportedly touches Stephen Bannon, Roger Stone
It has been 10 months since Fox News forced out CEO Roger Ailes after dozens of women accused him of sexual harassment - and other than paying $45 million i...

Politics Huffpost
Fox News Seriously Downplayed The James Comey News. It Backfired.
Fox News' primetime hosts downplayed or dismissed the huge political fallout Tuesday night following reports that President Donald Trump asked then-FBI Direct...

 **Fox News is grasping at straws to defend Trump: Punchlines** USA Today

Trevor Noah Criticizes "Aggressively Ignorant" Fox News for Coverage of James Comey's Trump Memo The Hollywood Reporter

THIS IS NOT NORMAL
DON'T EVEN PRETEND THIS IS NORMAL

90

Crispy Chaos Calamari

Ingredients

3 cups Vegetable oil
1/4 cup Flour
1 teaspoon Salt
1 teaspoon dried Oregano
1 dash of Garlic powder
1/2 teaspoon Black Pepper
12 squid, sliced into rings
1 Lemon - cut into wedges, for garnish

Directions

Pull up a seat and have some Crispy Chaos Calamari while you watch the many tentacles of chaos unfold

Preheat oil in a heavy, deep frying pan or pot. In a medium size mixing bowl mix together flour, salt, oregano and black pepper. Dredge squid through flour and spice mixture.
Place squid in oil for 2 to 3 minutes or until light brown.

Chris Murphy @ChrisMurphyCT · Mar 2
Your regular reminder that at the center of this engima wrapped in a riddle tucked inside a mystery are the tax returns.

Politics Newsweek
President Trump's shutdown threat creates a no-win situation for Republicans
Republicans, Democrats and outside experts agree that there's little political logic to the Trump White House's threat to shut down the government this week because it insists...

Video: Congress, White House try to strike budget deal as government shutdown looms
ABC News

Is wall funding worth a government shutdown?
CNN

Politics McClatchy Washington Bureau
Trump is being sued for saying 'Get 'em out of here' at a rally. He just did it again.
"Get them out of here." Those five words have already led to a lawsuit against President Donald Trump. But Trump continued to use them Saturday night at a...

Hasan Minhaj Makes Brutal, Biting Swipes at Trump During White House...

Watch Hasan Minhaj Roast Donald Trump And The Media At The White House...

Republicans are still happy with their leader "shaking things up" and continue to pledge their undying support, no matter what.

Democrats are astonished at how chaotic the Trump Administration has become...and (you guessed it) don't seem to be able to do anything about it.

Reprehensible Ravioli

Racism, bigotry and corruption tear apart the fabric of society and erode positive social norms. Cowardly vandalism and hate crimes are a sign of an ignorant, deteriorating society.

Social norms or mores are the rules of behavior that are considered acceptable in a group or society. People who do not follow these **norms** may be shunned or suffer some kind of consequence. **Norms** change according to the environment or situation and may change or be modified over time.

FUN FACT

Bernie Sanders @Sen... · 21h
It's healthy for people to disagree, but it's not healthy for a president to consistently lie. That's demagoguery.

Analysis | President Trump's first 100 days: The fact chec...
washingtonpost.com

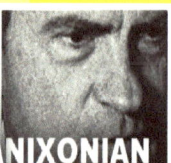

Politics — The Huffington Post
Trump's Sacking Of James Comey Is A Test For Republicans
Archibald Cox, special prosecutor for the Watergate investigation, issued a warning after President Richard Nixon ordered his removal in October 1973. "Whether we shall continue t...

James Comey's fall — CNN
Live: Reactions to President Trump's firing of FBI Director James Comey — Yahoo News

NIXONIAN

NEWS
Racist coward with poor grammar sends hateful note to family in Longmont
Kyle Clark, KUSA
2 minutes ago

Politics — The Independent
Donald Trump 'asked FBI director James Comey to consider imprisoning reporters'
Donald Trump told James Comey he should consider trying to imprison journalists for publishing classified information, it has been claimed. The request surfaced in a Ne...

Trump Trade Fades amid Political Debacle: What's the Impact? — Market Realist
 Where Russia Is Seen as a Buffer Against the U.S. — The Atlantic

Politics — HuffPost
Democrats Look To Close Conflict-Of-Interest Loophole Linked To Betsy DeVos
WASHINGTON — Democrats introduced legislation on Wednesday to close a conflict-of-interest loophole that was spotlighted after President Donald Trump...

U.S. — Cosmopolitan
Prison Time for Racist Threats at Child's Birthday
Victim of Georgia birthday party threats: How do I explain racism to kids? — CNN

FUN FACT
This is 2017

Shaun King
May 13 at 9:24pm · Facebook Mentions

This rally of white supremacists with torches aiming to intimidate the Black community in Charlottesville Virginia was not in 1957. This was tonight, in 2017.

This is where our country is going right now.

👍 Like Page

Politics — Yahoo News UK
Donald Trump accused of 'witness intimidation'
Donald Trump has been accused of trying to intimidate a witness who was set to testify at a hearing about possible Russian interference in the US election. Former acting Attorney...

 Sean Spicer calls Sally Yates a 'political opponent' in explaining why Trump ignored her advice — Business Insider
 Ted Cruz Tried To Corner Sally Yates On The Law. He Failed. — The Huffington Post

NowThis @nowthisnews · 1h
This congressman called for Trump to be impeached – and Trump supporters responded by threatening to lynch him

Sources: Russian officials bragged they could use Flynn to influence Trump
Russian officials bragged in conversations during the presidential campaign that they had cultivated a strong relationship with former Trump adviser retired Gen. Michael Flynn...
May 19, 2017
Tweeted by Richard W. Pai...

"we're gonna give you a short trial before we hang your n****r ass."

RECORDING OF CALL MADE TO REP. AL GREEN

92

Reprehensible Ravioli

Ingredients

- Cheese/Spinach Ravioli
- Tomato Basil Spaghetti sauce
- Shredded Parmesan Cheese
- Fresh Basil Leaves
- Fresh Oregano Leaves
- Smoked Paprika
- Garlic Powder
- Chili Powder
- Cayenne Powder
- Crushed Red Pepper

If your behavior has been reprehensible, make some Ravioli - they might actually forgive you (but don't count on it)

Directions

Boil 6 cups of water, add frozen ravioli, reduce to medium and cook until tender (about 8 min). Strain and set aside. Brown lean hamburg or "alternative" meat. Add tomato sauce and spices, heat on medium and add ravioli. Add a little agave or honey to sauce if desired. Garnish with shredded Parmesan cheese and fresh basil leaves.

News The Independent
White police officer shoots off-duty black officer in St Louis
A black off-duty police officer has been shot by a white colleague who "feared for his safety" in the US. The St Louis Metropolitan Police Department described the shooting as a "friendl...

 White St. Louis police officer shoots off-duty black officer
CBS News

 An off-duty black cop tried to help stop an ongoing crime. A white officer shot him.
Miami Herald

Politics ThinkProgress
The racist, discredited argument Trump's DOJ just made in a federal court
Who knew something like this could happen with Jeff Sessions in charge? Here's a pro tip for the lawyers at Jeff Sessions' Justice Department: If you want to defend the president's effort...

 The Latest: Attorney: Travel ban is religiously motivated
Associated Press

 Trump travel ban defence met with protest
BBC News

Politics Business Insider
Details leaked about the White House's upcoming education budget include proposals to cut science programs and student...
The White House's 2018 budget for education - expected to be released next week as part of the administration's full spending proposals - appears to double down on the eye-popping...

 Trump's first education budget: Deep public school cuts in pursuit of school choice
Chicago Tribune

 Trump's Education Department Budget May Cut Student Loan Forgiveness Program
International Business Times

Republicans remain loyal to their fearless leader, but a few have discretely stashed their red hats and "Make America Great Again" T-Shirts in the bottom drawer....just for the time being...

Democrats are trying to form support groups and are encouraged to attend weekly therapy sessions. It's getting pretty ugly out there...

Impeachment Cobbler

Impeachment

From Wikipedia, the free encyclopedia

This article is about a step in the removal of a public official. For challenging a witness in a legal proceeding, see witness impeachment.

Impeachment is the process by which a legislative body formally levels charges against a high official of Government. Impeachment does not necessarily mean removal from office; it is only a formal statement of charges, akin to an indictment in criminal law, and is thus only the first step towards removal. Once an individual is impeached, he or she must then face the possibility of conviction via legislative vote, which then entails the removal of the individual from office.

Now that Donald Trump is the President, his opponents, and even his allies, have impeachment on their minds. With Trump's impeachment odds changing with seemingly every ALL CAPS tweet he puts online, discussion of whether the 45th president of the United States will be impeached for any number of reasons continues to flow among people on both sides of the aisle.

Trump's support from Congressional Republicans is a mile wide and an inch deep. If they turn on him, they can and will impeach him, even if the legal case is relatively weak. If they don't, they won't vote to impeach him even if the case is strong. That's how it works.

At the end of the day, grounds for impeachment is pretty much whatever Congress says it is. If Congress wants to get there, the paths are open.

FUN FACTS

Business Corruption and Conflicts of Interest • War Crimes • Renewed Sexual Assault Allegations • Sharing Confidential Information With His Relatives • Perjury and other forms of lying • Corrupt Business Entanglements

Impeachment Cobbler

Ingredients

- 1/2 cup melted Butter
- 1 cup Flour
- 1 cup sugar
- 2 teaspoons Baking Powder
- 1/4 teaspoon Salt
- 2/3 cup Milk
- 1 Egg
- 1 can sliced Peaches,
- 1 cup Sugar
- 1 teaspoon Cinnamon
- 1/2 teaspoon Nutmeg

Impeachment never tasted so sweet!

Directions

Melt butter in a 9 x 13 inch pan.
Mix together flour, sugar, baking powder & salt.
Stir in milk & egg.
Pour evenly over melted butter.
Combine peaches, sugar & spices and spread over batter-DO NOT STIR!
Bake 35-45 minutes at 350°F until batter comes to the top and is golden brown.
Serve warm with ice cream.

Bottom Line →

"The question is no longer whether there are grounds to impeach Trump," Reich said. "The practical question is whether there is the political will."

"As long as Republicans remain in the majority in the House (where a bill of Impeachment originates), it's unlikely," he said.

Politics International Business Times

Odds Grow For Possible Trump Impeachment

A U.K. betting house "didn't even offer odds on Obama being impeached or resigning, which speaks volumes about the...

FUN FACT

Republicans wanted to impeach Bill Clinton over a sex scandal, but don't think Trump should be impeached with several sex-scandals, law suits, countless lies and deception and/or unlawful Russian ties.

Democrats feel that an impeachment is warranted for several documented reasons....but don't seem to be able to do anything about it, with the GOP holding the majority.

Meanwhile Mojitos

Yellowstone supervolcano hit by a swarm of more than 230 earthquakes in one week
Yellowstone supervolcano has been hit by a series of earthquakes, with more 30 recorded since June 12.
YAHOO.COM

Gizmodo @Gizmodo · 3h
The White House science division officially has zero staff members
gizmo.do/GTDC42o

Meanwhile...
China is poised to lead the global Green Energy production industry. Canada legalizes Marijuana which increases jobs and revenue. Paris Agreement (international climate change coalition w/o the USA) strives to move towards green energy efforts.

The government wants everyone's personal information and voting history. Most states are refusing.

NPR @NPR · 20h
The White House voter fraud commission wants data from all 50 states by July 14, five days before its first meeting.

3h
Everyone should be registered as "unaffiliated." Vote on individual issues, such as ousting tyranny.

Science Yahoo News
Massive crack in Antarctic ice shelf grows 11 miles in 6 days, potentially creating world's largest iceberg
According to NASA, IceBridge scientists measured the Larsen C fracture to be about 70 miles long, more than 300 feet wide and about a third of a mile deep. In the six days...

BBC News (World) @BBCWorld · 2h
Hawaiian Hokule'a canoe makes it round the world

You Retweeted
David V. Thomas, Jr. @VaughnAsset · Apr 20
Scientists in the U.K. have created a graphene filter that makes seawater drinkable. Newsweek has details:

Pablo Rodas-Martini @pablorodas · 8m
#CLIMATE #p2 RT Tackling the plastic bottle crisis and our wider disregard for nature | Letters divr.it/PRHWcc #tlot #ccot

Hawaiian Hokule'a canoe makes it round the world - BBC New
The traditional Polynesian boat completed the three-year trip with modern navigation instruments.
bbc.co.uk

Graphene sieve makes seawater drinkable
Scientists have figured out how to use the 'wonder material' graphene to desalinate seawater.
newsweek.com

Greenpeace Retweeted
Energydesk @Energydesk · Jun 29
Breaking: Landmark industry funded study shows pesticide risk to honey b
bit.ly/2t9yC8D

NPR @NPR · 1h
The Texas Supreme Court ruled against extending benefits policies to married same-sex couples in the state

Texas Supreme Court Rules Against Benefits For Same-Se...
The case challenges the fact that Houston's benefits policy, which is

World Mashable
Here's why you should pay close attention to India's space program
While India's space agency may not be the first organization you think about when it comes to space travel, there are many reasons we should all be...

Meanwhile Mojitos

Ingredients

2 tablespoons Lime Juice
1 teaspoon Agave
1 cup crushed ice
12 fresh Mint leaves, plus 5 small sprigs for garnish
1/4 cup White Rum
2 tablespoons Club Soda

Ahhhh! Such a refreshing change from national news. maybe it's best to turn off the TV for a while...

Directions

In 10-ounce glass, stir together lime juice and Agave until dissolved. Add 1/4 cup crushed ice. Rub mint leaves over rim of glass, then tear leaves in half and add to glass. Stir, then add rum, remaining crushed ice, and club soda. Stir, then tuck mint sprigs into top of glass and enjoy!

Gizmodo @Gizmodo · 2h
Wonder Woman is now the DCEU's most successful movie in the US
gizmo.do/a1FzduM

The Senate's Health Care Bill Remains Shrouded in Secrecy
The Senate is closing in on a health care bill that could affect millions of Americans and overhaul an industry that makes up one-sixth of the economy. There's one problem: almost...

No States Support The American Health Care Act [Infographic]

Health Care Declassified: Behind the Senate's secrecy

Science · BGR News
Five asteroids will cruise by Earth in the next year, and one is coming very close
The handful of asteroids, which are thought to be as small as 8 meters in diameter to as large as 90 meters, will all pass within five lunar distances. One lunar distance is the...

Sound Fire Extinguisher Drops the Bass to Put Out Flames - YouTube

https://www.youtube.com/watch?v=cSX9eR8Mles
Apr 14, 2015 - Uploaded by NerdAlert
How can dropping that bass actually help and save people? Two engineers invented a way to **put out fires** ...

FUN FACT

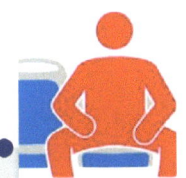

World · Mashable
Manspreading is now banned on public transit in Madrid for the good of humanity
In the wake of warnings against manspreading on display in public transit facilities around the world, The Municipal Transportation Company in Madri...

Madrid cracks down on 'manspreading' on public transport
BBC News

Manspreading: Public bus signs tell men to keep legs together
USA Today

Yeah, THAT happened - Mens Rompers. So glad I grew up when I did. OMG...

Republicans think Mojitos are not so bad.

Democrats think Mojitos are pretty good.

97

Progressives Paradise Pizza

Natasha Geiling Follow
Reporter at ThinkProgress. Contact me: ngeiling@americanprogress.org
Mar 27 · 4 min read

Clean energy employs more people than fossil fuels in nearly every U.S. state

Trump's upcoming executive order meant to boost fossil fuel jobs may end up harming an even bigger job creator — renewable energy.

Bernie Sanders would have used those $96M WASTED IN MISSILES into education, health care, infrastructure, clean energy ... JOBS

U.S. Yahoo News Photo Staff
People's Climate March across the U.S.
Thousands of people across the U.S. are marching on President Donald Trump's hundredth day in office to demand action on climate change. In Washington, D....

 Environmental protesters swarm outside White House as Trump hits milestone — Reuters

 Protesters To Mark Trump's First 100 Days With Boston Common Rally — CBS Boston

Progressive Paradise Pizza

Ingredients

- Thin Pizza Crust
- Garlic Olive Oil or
- Alfredo sauce
- Pesto
- Spinach
- Artichoke Hearts
- Black Olives
- Red Onion

- Feta Cheese
- Mozzarella Cheese
- Minced Garlic
- Garlic Powder
- Oregano
- Sage
- Black Pepper

Directions

Nourish your body and soul with Progressive Paradise Pizza. Imagine everyone having heathcare, an education - a world powered by green energy (don't choke on the cheese)

Spread the pizza crust, spoon out the olive oil and/or Alfredo sauce. Sprinkle the seasonings over the sauce, then add the rest of the ingredients to taste. Bake this delightful masterpiece in the oven at 425° for 15 minutes.
You can't go wrong, if it's green!

Today's Energy Jobs Are in Solar, Not Coal

By NADJA POPOVICH   APRIL 25, 2017

Republicans are glad Trump is rolling back corporate regulations and EPA standards and focusing on fossil fuels. They are also OK with how Trump opted-out of the Paris Accord.

Democrats still envision a progressive nation that embraces clean energy, education, affordable healthcare, equal rights, bi-partisan cooperation/maturity and progressive international relations.

Corporate Coalition Coffee

NatureFresh™ Farms @Nature_Fresh · 21h
Being a good #corporate citizen means taking part in #community events that give back. It all starts in our schools: ow.ly/KUOE30csZRS

Barack Obama follows

Economic Democracy = Political Democracy

Corporate Social Responsibility

TrainingZone @TrainingZone · May 23
Community blog: A Strategy to Move to an Engaged Corporate Culture >

A Strategy to Move to an Engaged Corporate Culture
The workplace has changed drastically over the last few years. This is partially due to digital disruption, but also because the employer-employee relationsh
trainingzone.co.uk

FUN FACT

COUNTRY	RATIO OF PAY CEO VS. AVG WORKER
JAPAN	11:1
GERMANY	12:1
FRANCE	15:1
ITALY	20:1
CANADA	20:1
SOUTH AFRICA	21:1
BRITAIN	22:1
MEXICO	47:1
VENEZUELA	50:1
UNITED STATES	475:1

THE BIGGEST 5 OIL COMPANIES MADE 135 BILLION IN PROFIT LAST YEAR
Chevron bp conoco shell Exxon Mobil
WHY IN THE WORLD ARE WE GIVING THEM AT LEAST 10 BILLION IN SUBSIDIES WHILE WE ARE CLOSING PUBLIC SCHOOLS?
Storm is Coming

S&P Global ✓ @SPGlobal
Mike Chinn, President for @SPGMarketIntel volunteered alongside his colleagues at @CHT1973 to build a garden for campers #SPGlobalimpact

Zimpapers Digital @Zimpapers · May 26
Corporate Affairs Manager @BTonhodzayi said the donation was the **corporate**'s way of giving back to the **community** which the business operates

100

Corporate Coalition Coffee

Ingredients

- 1 Cup Fresh Brewed Coffee
- GMO free creamer
- Raw Agave (to taste)
- Ground Clove (pinch)
- Ground Cinnamon (pinch)
- Fresh Mint Leaves

Nothing tastes quite as good as Coalition

Directions

Brew a fresh pot of coffee. Add the spices and cream as desired. Stir and garnish with a mint sprig.

Reflect on the idea of how strong a nation and peoples could be with a corporate coalition (or at least paying their fair share and avoiding loop holes).

Republicans are currently trying to roll back corporate regulations, EPA standards and funding for community services, while giving huge tax breaks to corporations and the wealthy, hoping the "trickle down" theory will actually work this time.

Democrats feel that corporations that engage and invest in the communities that built them, pave the way to a mutually successful nation, built on fiscal responsibility, true pride and patriotism.

101

Whirled Peas

Heartwarming

I am so proud of the truly decent and conscientious Americans that stand up against bigotry, racism, sexism, and other injustices.

I hope we continue to fight to protect the good people of America and the environment.

#OURVOICESAREVITAL — GREENPEACE

Imagine ~

Imagine all nations banding together to save the ecosystem... and each other.

STAND-UP FOR WORLD PEACE

Discover Magazine @DiscoverMag · 17h
In Detroit, bumblebees make a comeback: bit.ly/2rmTXvX

Rudaw English @RudawEnglish · Jun 8
Women in Kurdistan march through the night for world peace
rudaw.net/english/cultur...

This is what leadership in the face of authoritarianism looks like. The United States is no longer the leader of the free world. Vive la France.

 Elizabeth Warren
I LOVE the Boston Pride Parade. It shows our Commonwealth and our country at its best.

Dancing (not walking) in the Boston Pride Parade

Macron calls out Russian propaganda while standing next to Putin
"I will not give an inch on this," the French president said in a joint press conference.
NYDAILYNEWS.COM

Cooperation for the good of the many

102

Whirled Peas

Ingredients

1 packet Lentils (per person)
3 Tablespoons Hemp Seeds
2 Tablespoons shredded Parmesan Cheese
Smoked Paprika (pinch or two)
Turmeric (pinch or two)
Chili Powder (pinch or two)
Garlic Powder (pinch or two)
Crushed Red Pepper (pinch)
Fresh Oregano leaves
Hemp Oil (drizzle)

Envision world peace as you enjoy this healthy blend of natural goodness.

Directions

Heat Lentil pouch as directed (1min microwave)
Pour contents into microwave-safe bowl, add seasoning and stir in.
Top surface with hemp seeds, then top the center with Parmesan cheese
Sprinkle Oregano leaves in the center and drizzle hemp oil in a swirl
Microwave again for 30 seconds to a minute.
It's good stuff! - And so satisfying!

Love and compassion are the pillars of **world peace**
HH #DalaiLama #love

Republicans prefer to be well armed and use the lion's share of funds for military weapons.

Democrats feel that the USA has more than enough military mite and prefer to use the lion's share of funds for the citizens; infrastructure, education, environment, healthcare and community services.

Wrap Up

Be Informed - Consider the Source(s) - Participate!

The Take-Aways...
- Just remember, assholes come in every color...
- Integrity does still exist
- Be informed, check your sources & participate!
- Corporate Community Coalition = Strong Economy, Strong
- Corporations & Strong Communities = A Strong Nation
- Use basic decency & understanding
- Try not to be part of the problem
- Treat everyone as you would want to be treated
- Trade Places, Trade Faces, 'Walk a Mile' - COMPASSION!

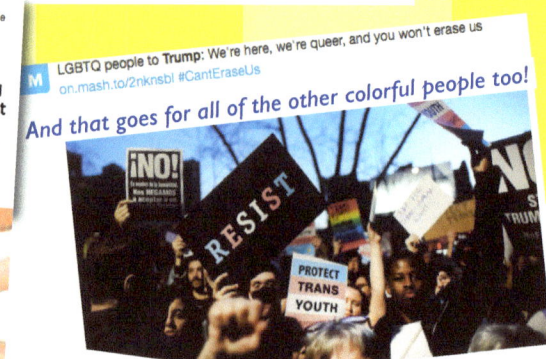

FOLLOW THE LEADER: HOW 11 COUNTRIES ARE SHIFTING TO RENEWABLE ENERGY   FUN FACT

Who's embracing wind? Solar? Geothermal? These countries could provide blueprints for the worldwide shift to renewable energy.

This December, almost 200 countries from every corner of the world signed the Paris Agreement, committing to decrease greenhouse gas emissions and – dare we say – *save the world!*

The question on everyone's mind: *How?*

The truth is, we don't have to wait on scientists to invent some newfangled contraption. The solutions are already here! **We simply need to ramp up renewable energy generation, and fast.**

The Leaders of Renewable Energy
1. Sweden 99%   2. Costa Rica 99%   3. Nicaragua 54%
4. Scotland 97%   5. Germany 78%   6. Uruguay 95%

Wrap Up

Ingredients

Large Flour Tortilla
(Spinach, tomato, plain)
Lettuce, Kale
Purple Cabbage
Diced Tomatoes
Avocado

Red Onion
Meat, Tofu, WHATEVER!

Add whatever you want!
..it's a free country...

Enjoy this diverse and healthy combination of delights

Directions

Lay the tortilla out flat.
Put the leafy ingredients over half of the tortilla, leaving an inch or so at one end of the tortilla. Add all of the other ingredients on top of the leafy layer. Drizzle olive oil, pesto or salad dressing over the ingredients. Gently fold the side that has all of the ingredients on it, while tucking in the uncovered part of the tortilla as you roll.

You could just roll the tortilla without tucking in one end, but the contents may fall out as you eat it, but thats all OK too - "Its all good" ...it's a free country. The main point of this dish is to enjoy the diversity of ingredients and flavors.

Authors around the world stand up for free speech and forests
Blog entry by Kat Clark | 31 May, 2017

Authors, journalists, poets and playwrights know that every time the right words are put to paper, or typed to a screen, our planet gets a little better. Because, without the right to express ourselves freely, we cannot make that...

 CBB @CBB_Community · May 11
@BeyondBank Growing expectation from consumers for **corporate** social responsibility and sustainability.

Politics *The Independent*
Donald Trump's friend Howard Stern says 'nobody wanted Hillary Clinton to win more than Donald Trump'
Howard Stern has argued nobody was more keen for Hillary Clinton to win than Donald Trump himself. The radio personality, who is America's most notorious shock jock, said President...

 Clinton to launch 'resistance' PAC
CNN

 Hillary Clinton is ready for her comeback tour

Republicans may or may not agree with (or understand) the "Strength in Diversity" concept and they prefer capitalism with no "hand-outs!" They prefer above all, a strong military, fossil fuels and religion over education, with no separation of church and state. (ironically much like Iran)

Democrats believe in inclusion and equal rights. They believe in education, healthcare and renewable energy. They believe America is the land of immigrants and was founded with the help of the original inhabitants who offered their food, knowledge and compassion. (ironically Native Americans may regret this)

The Boil Down

Things can be complicated, with a lot of variables and view points, but positive social norms and common decency can keep things in check. Six months into the Trump presidency has many of us questioning the stability of those "norms." Some people choose to operate above the law (more so below) and feel they are "entitled."

When law enforcement and elected officials operate above the law, it is a sign of a crumbling society—eroding from the inside out. When the supreme example of law and order can be described as "thug-like," the delicately woven fabric of society will be torn apart.

Mainstream media continues to air a majority of TV shows that are centered around guns and violence. **Every single day, throughout the day, we are shown guns being used to solve nearly every situation.** We can see this behavior being reflected in "real life" as gun sales increase along with gun related incidents throughout the nation. At this point social evolution seems to be rolling backwards and we asking, "How did this happen?"

The 2016 campaign shocked (and horrified) a lot of people. We had not previously witnessed such a display of politics and bad behavior. It seemed as though a new, lower level of "politicing" was becoming the new norm.

One of the other products of this new norm, was a new, higher level of communication between the POTUS and his supporters and anyone who chose to "follow" his comments on Twitter. The Mainstream Media (MSM) was quick to report any, and all comments emitted from Trump and his administration - of which, there seems to be no shortage. Ironically, with this higher volume of communication, we find a lack of substance and truth as White House correspondents often offered nothing but dodged questions and smoke screens...lots of smoke, and where there is smoke, there is usually fire.

Most of the ingredients for this project were captured in 'real time.' There was a constant barrage of headlines and tweets. I captured only a fraction of the daily whirlwind of news and commentary. For the sake of my sanity, I wrapped it up and published the first edition by July 4th 2017.

FUN FACT

At this time during Obama's first 100 days, he was being lambasted for using Dijon mustard on a hotdog that he bought from a local shop. I don't know why FOX news thought this was bad enough (or important enough) to do a story on, but it goes to show differing view points.

Whatever your particular view point, and no matter how this turns out, I hope, if nothing else, this little cookbook demonstrates the need to seek out the **facts**, consider the source and explore other points of view.

Compassion

PARTICIPATE

*Trade places to gain perspective.
I mean REALLY try to imagine it.*

*Imagine you are suddenly black, white, red, yellow, pink,
orange, male, female, gay, old, disabled, poor....
Would things be different?*

*Participate to help any and all Presidents
direct our government that is*
for the people, by the people.

Look for <u>Recipes for Disaster</u>, Volume 2 to be published October 2019

www.ingramcontent.com/pod-product-compliance
Lightning Source LLC
Chambersburg PA
CBHW041152290426
44108CB00002B/49